The Gospel of John

The Gospel of John

A Thematic Approach

R. JACKSON PAINTER
FOREWORD BY GERALD BORCHERT

WIPF & STOCK · Eugene, Oregon

THE GOSPEL OF JOHN
A Thematic Approach

Wipf & Stock
An Imprint of Wipf and Stock Publishers
199 W. 8th Ave., Suite 3
Eugene, OR 97401
www.wipfandstock.com

ISBN 13: 978-1-60899-484-7

Manufactured in the U.S.A.

For Lynn

Contents

Foreword

THE GOSPEL OF JOHN is one of the most loved books in the Bible and it contains some of the best known verses in Scripture. Indeed, while the text of John is easy to read even in Greek, the Johannine ideas are exceedingly complex and can readily be viewed in simplistic terms. So, what is the best way to develop an adequate understanding of this gospel?

For years I have insisted that employing a thematic approach to the gospel enables the student of the Bible to gain a more holistic understanding of this book and to assist in forestalling the common practice of reasserting ones preconceptions of what the evangelist is in fact saying. Painter has learned this lesson well and has emerged as an exceedingly competent interpreter of John. His choice of the meta-themes of "Revelation and Response" provide an excellent working basis for reflecting on the individual themes of "Identity," "Life," "Festival," "Witness," "Believing," "Signs" and "Destiny."

He understands the nature of living with tension that is evident in John's Gospel as is eminently clear from his discussion on "Destiny." And he does not fall into the trap of asserting a "realized eschatology" but has opted for a far more authentic picture of interweaving the present or "now" with the future or "the coming" in a so-called "continuous" understanding of time that is present in John. He also does not succumb to isolating John 3:16 and the concept of God's love from its context of God's demand for an adequate response, as is frequently done by some people.

While many interpreters bifurcate the gospel in terms of the presence of "Signs" in John, Painter's interpretation has tied the signs to the great sign of the Cross and Resurrection and thus has given a much more significant meaning to the Cleansing of the Temple pericope in John 2 and led to a more holistic understanding of this theme.

His use of the Johannine Questions as a important key to interpreting the Johannine themes is strategic because it enables him to articulate the various options in the answers that are suggested by the questions. As a result his presentation of the themes is rich with depth as the reader is led to consider the reality of those options.

Moreover, in teaching the Gospel of John I have always been intrigued in listening to my students as they present their papers that many of them think that the theme they have discussed is the most pervasive in the gospel. Such remarks only point to the fact that the evangelist was a genius in the interweaving of his themes about Jesus in this gospel. In discussing each of the seven chosen themes, Painter constantly connects each theme to other themes in the gospel and thus is true to the fact that no theme can be studied in isolation from the other themes.

In concluding his work, Painter has also provided several models for students in how to study texts from the gospel in terms of its themes.

From the above comments, it should be clear that I have found reading this book by Dr. Jack Painter to be extremely rewarding. Although he has not filled the book with multiple footnotes as one might find in a major commentary, it is clear that he has read widely and has taken into account the major discussions among scholars on the issues involved in Johannine studies. Accordingly, his perspectives are based on seasoned reflection and are both balanced and insightful. It has therefore been a genuine pleasure to write this Forward for one who previously was my very perceptive graduate assistant and helped me with the research for the first volume of my commentary on John and who has since emerged as an extremely competent interpreter of the Gospel of John.

To you the reader of this work, I heartily commend this book on the themes of John. While it may be smaller in comparison to some other works on John, the number of pages is hardly a test of its significance. You should find this interpretive book to be both a very readable and an extremely enlightening tool for better understanding the thinking of why Clement of Alexandria early called this book "the Spiritual Gospel."

Gerald L. Borchert, PhD, LLB
Retired Dean and Professor of New Testament

Preface

*T*HE GOSPEL OF JOHN: *A Thematic Approach* identifies seven themes that John weaves together to form the rich theological tapestry of his gospel. The book grows out of my experiences teaching the Gospel of John over the last fifteen years at the Alliance Biblical Seminary in Manila (now Alliance Graduate School) and most recently at Simpson University. The idea of treating John thematically comes from Gerald Borchert, my doctoral supervisor, who taught Johannine themes in his seminary course. His influence has left a deep mark on how I view and approach the entire New Testament. The years of interaction with my students and their thematic papers have served to sharpen my thought regarding these Johannine themes. Though footnotes are scarce, discerning readers will detect the influence of a number of Johannine scholars, especially C. H. Dodd, Rudolph Bultmann, Raymond Brown, C. K. Barrett, John Ashton, Craig Koester, Robert Kysar, Jerome Neyrey, and Gerald Borchert.

My hope and passion is that this book will provide students an accessible approach to the gospel of John in the classroom and for a life of self-study and ministry. Simply put, I desire for students, pastors, and others interested in John to see the big picture of how John "works." I not only want to show what the big ideas are in John, but how John actually incorporates those ideas into this unique gospel. Commentaries and historical-critical studies of the Gospel of John abound which treat the background, philology and theology of John. In recent years the narrative approaches have also helped students to develop a deeper understanding of the way the gospel was written. The studies of Dodd, Koester and others treat thematic elements in the gospels but more from a symbolic perspective. Their studies are centered on symbolic motifs and background issues; in addition they address an advanced audience.

The key approach in this book is to show how symbols and motifs are set within larger "themes" and "meta-themes" and so can be seen as threads throughout the gospel despite a change of vocabulary or image. In the spirit of Kysar's excellent volume, *John, The Maverick Gospel*, I hope that this book will help the aspiring student of John to gain an "eye" for the gospel as he or she reads and studies. Even more than what Kysar does, I want the student of John's gospel to have a facility in reading any passage with reasonable understanding because of having read this book.

While historical-critical issues may occasionally be alluded to, this study is first and foremost a literary study that seeks to understand the distinctive way that John writes his theological story of Jesus. As such this study is best used as a complement to commentaries and other studies. After learning and appropriating the thematic approach to John, one should be able to read and study John with a newly developed facility.

The reader of this book should certainly not presuppose any sort of anti-historical bias. I have followed very closely the "John, Jesus, and History" seminar at the Society of Biblical literature over the last decade and wholeheartedly applaud the efforts to bring balance to the history and theology debate in John. This study is simply attempting to address the theological literary strategy as it exists without any comment on historical issues. I personally get as excited as anyone when I stand at the Pool of Bethesda or the recently excavated Pool of Siloam in Jerusalem. History comes alive. But as exhilarating as history may be, John is not so concerned with events as the person of the events: Jesus. John's concern is with the "Word become flesh."

I need to stress that throughout the book, unless otherwise stated, the *text* of John is always in view, not the events *behind* the text. I will neither make any critical judgments with regard to the words of Jesus or for any other speaker in the gospel for that matter. To write, "Jesus says" simply states that John narratively portrays Jesus as speaking those words. Scholars have long agreed that John has shaped the Jesus speech in the gospel to a certain extent. This study acknowledges but does not enter into that debate.

A pedagogical purpose guides the structure of the book. The introduction serves to present the thematic approach to the Gospel of John with appropriate groundwork and definitions. Part One treats each Johannine theme through succinct essays. The essays do not seek to be exhaustive, but do seek to adequately trace and explain the theme so that the student can recognize the theme in any passage of John. I encourage the reader to mark a copy of John with colored pencils, one for each theme, while working through each chapter. Part Two gives examples of how the themes work together in the text through an examination of several selected sections in the gospel. Hopefully this organization will enhance the usefulness of the book in the classroom, in personal study and in sermon preparation. Throughout the book, translations from the New Testament are mine, unless otherwise noted.

My earnest desire is that by seeing John through thematic eyes, the reader will encounter the message of John in an ever clearer and life-changing way.

A note for preachers: Using the thematic approach to John can be a fruitful way of planning sermons on John. I have four possible suggestions. One is to prepare a series of sermons corresponding to each of the themes. A second is to focus on one theme for a series of sermons with each sermon corresponding to a motif or related motifs in the theme (along the lines of the headings in each chapter). A third is to preach through a section of John using a thematic analysis such as those illustrated in Part 2. A fourth way would be to use the gospel summaries in the appendix as texts that form the basis of one or more sermons.

I want to thank my students at Simpson University and the A. W. Tozer Theological Seminary who have borne with my continual rehearsal of Johannine themes in their classes. The most recent Tozer class and Linda Jackson read the initial draft and gave me very useful feedback. I also want to express appreciation to Jerry Borchert who read the manuscript and gave valuable comments. To Beth Venugopal, I want to say, "I finally wrote the book!" Lastly, I want to thank my dear wife, Lynn, and children, Emily, Daniel, and Joanna, who have encouraged me and patiently endured my constant trips to the office to write.

Abbreviations

Gk.	Greek
Heb.	Hebrew
LXX	Septuagint (the Greek OT)
NASB	New American Standard Bible
NRSV	New Revised Standard Version
NEB	New English Bible
NT	New Testament
OT	Old Testament

Introduction

Revelation and Response

THE GOSPEL OF JOHN is *the* gospel for many people, or at least their favorite gospel. The simple language, the compelling stories, and the clear message about the identity of Jesus and the need to believe make John a beloved gospel. In this book, I want to help you to understand *how* John uses language to create the clear gospel message about Jesus Christ.

Have you ever noticed that the Gospel of John is full of questions? There are about 170 of them, or an average of eight questions per chapter. Most of the questions are about two things: Who is Jesus? and Do you (or why don't you) believe? The Gospel of John not only asks these questions but boldly provides the answers. John sets out to accomplish two things in his gospel account. He wants to declare who Jesus is as the very revelation of God and he wants people to respond to this Jesus in a life-altering way, resulting in what he terms as "born of God." In each chapter in Part One, I begin with an actual question in John, and show how John answers the question through a distinctive theme.

THE LANGUAGE OF JOHN

The Gospel of John uses deceptively simple language. John's fairly limited vocabulary results in a distinctive and easily recognizable style. Terms such as light, life, believe, know, witness, truth, love and others occur throughout the gospel and even the letters of John. The repetition of these words serves to create a comfortable environment for novice readers of the gospel as they encounter the terms in different settings throughout the work. John's message, however, is far from simplistic. The simple language is configured in a way which leads to multiple layers of meaning. At the micro level, John uses many words, even actions

1

and people, symbolically. Many of these terms repeat to form motifs. For example, the image of light develops into a motif when it recurs in a number of different contexts, as well as when contrasted with darkness.

But despite a certain inherent dynamism, images and motifs do not in themselves do justice to the larger literary and theological plan of John. At a macro level, John distributes a series of *themes* throughout the gospel that he intertwines in a variety of ways that mutually illumine each other. The themes in most cases include images and motifs, but are not limited to them. For example, the Life theme identifies Jesus as life-giving Savior, but John uses a variety of images (and their extended motifs) to illustrate this aspect of who he is, such as light, water, bread, and wine. John also includes acts such as Jesus' miraculous healings. None of these images or motifs comprises the theme alone, but together serve to present the larger idea of Jesus as life-giving Savior. Again, though "believe" may be the primary action of the Believing theme, many verbs function as vehicles that convey the movement toward Jesus.

DEFINITIONS: THEME, IMAGE, MOTIF

Some definitions are in order here. A "theme" as it is used in this book is a large idea suggested by a number of related images and motifs in the text. An "image" is an entity in the text that has a level of significance different than the literal sense of that entity.[1] A "motif" is a specific term or phrase (or a closely related term such as an opposite) that *recurs* throughout the text, such as the symbolic use of "his/my hour," or the phrase "I am," or the combination of terms Father and Son. An image may also be a motif if that image recurs. *For this treatment of John, a motif itself does not constitute a theme but is one of several terms or phrases that together point to a larger idea–the theme.* Multiple motifs for a theme add complexity to the theme and lead to numerous layers, nuances, and ultimately depth in the themes of the gospel and in their interaction with one another.

In addition, a number of images and motifs fit more than one theme, thus intensifying the complexity. This situation is abundantly evident in the Festival theme where items from the Identity, Life and Witness themes are drawing on Old Testament foundations. A prime example is the phrase, "I am the Bread from Heaven" which fits into Identity, Life and Festival themes simultaneously. Another instance is

---

1. An "image" in this sense is functionally equivalent to a "symbol." Unless otherwise noted, "symbol" and "image" are synonymous.

the Spirit motif. The Spirit appears as part of the Identity, Life, Witness and Destiny themes. Marking the text of John with a range of colors becomes a challenge in these instances!

"META-THEMES" IN JOHN

There are two overarching ideas in John, pointed out by numerous commentators, which I refer to as "meta-themes," Revelation and Response. A meta-theme for our purposes is one of the basic structural ideas in the gospel developed by the themes. The Gospel of John preeminently concerns the revelation of God in the person of Jesus Christ which calls for a response from those who encounter this revelation. In practical terms, however, the revelation aspect works out with regard to Jesus' identity, commonly called the Christology of John. The gospel writer is constantly addressing the question, "who is Jesus?" through statements of the narrator, through words of various characters and through words of Jesus himself. Whenever John addresses the question of identity, he also addresses the question "Do you believe?" to those in the gospel and to the reader. An encounter with the identity of Jesus demands a response. The so-called purpose statement of the gospel in 20:31 sets out this dual focus succinctly: "These things are written that you might believe that Jesus is the Christ the Son of God and that believing you might have life in his name." Earlier, John 3:16 makes the revelation of Jesus clear as well as the proper response: "For God loved the world in this way, that he gave his only Son, so that whoever believes in him should not perish but have eternal life." Out of this dual focus of Revelation and Response flow the themes which roughly correspond to one or the other of these two meta-themes. Indeed, an examination of the themes exposes the meta-themes, rather than an independent examination of the meta-themes. At least two themes (Witness and Destiny) strongly connect to both Revelation and Response and all of the themes have some points of correspondence with both.

THE STRUCTURE OF JOHN

John structures the gospel in two ways. First, he sets out the story of Jesus in a narrative, chronological sequence. Narrative studies of John give attention to diachronic features such as plot, change in setting, and character development.[2] Second, John creates the narrative with a synchronic theological structuring where all of the themes enter and exit again and again throughout the gospel. Indeed, though there is a narrative sequence to John, that sequence is composed of a series of episodes which can largely stand alone. Each episode includes most, or even all, of the themes. Each theme consists of a rich collection of words, images, and motifs that occur from beginning to end in the gospel. While each theme may develop weight as a result of repetition and variety, the themes scarcely change in terms of their basic concepts as introduced in the Prologue. The themes do intertwine with the other themes to create a multi-layered development of the meta-themes of Revelation and Response, but even here, the development is more of depth rather than extension. The genius of John is the way the gospel writer infuses the atemporal and spiritual framework of God's revelation of himself in Jesus Christ into a chronological narrative set within a historical framework.

DUALISM

One characteristic in the Gospel of John which permeates all of the themes to some extent is dualism, that is, the presence of various opposites in the gospel such as light and dark, above and below, present and future, good and evil, life and death, love and hate, etc.[3] Each theme has a positive focus as its main attribute, but the positive is always set in relief by its opposite. Thus, whereas Jesus' origin is from God (and those who believe in him), the origin of those who do not believe is the devil; the former are born from above, the latter from below; the former walk in the light, the latter in darkness; the former have life, the latter death. As each theme unfolds in the gospel John will often contrast the positive aspect of the theme with the negative.

THE THEMES

Here then briefly are each of the themes with its predominant meta-theme(s).[4] Though John does set the person of Jesus within a larger trini-

---

2. See quintessentially, Culpepper, *Anatomy of the Fourth Gospel.*

3. Philosophical dualism is not in view here, nor later Christological dualism.

4. Throughout the book, when I refer to a theme, the term will be capitalized, for example, Identity or Destiny. Otherwise, take the word in its normal sense (i.e. identity, destiny).

tarian frame, the themes focus primarily on the Son, whom John refers to initially as the *Logos*.

1. Identity (Revelation)

The Identity theme regards the divine origin and identity of Jesus, or in question form, "Where is Jesus from?" and "Who is Jesus?" Chief motifs of this theme are *Logos*, pre-existence, the Son in its various combinations, and the absolute "I am" sayings. The Identity theme is closely aligned with its parent meta-theme Revelation, but can be clearly articulated as a theme alongside the others in this category.

2. Life (Revelation)

The Life theme reveals Jesus as Savior. The most prominent motifs are light and life, with the corresponding negations darkness and death. Other symbolic images such as wine, water and bread, Jesus' acts of healing, and the Spirit are aspects of this rich theme. All of the "I am" statements with predicates fit this theme.

3. Festival (Revelation)

The Festival theme shows Jesus as the fulfillment of scripture and symbolically indicates Jesus as the fulfillment of everything Jewish. For instance, John sees Jesus as the fulfillment of the Jewish festivals for which the theme is named. But much more, Jesus is the expected Messiah; he completes and replaces the Law and its purity rituals; he replaces the Temple; he is greater than Abraham, Jacob and Moses; the Old Testament images of God are fulfilled in him. In addition, the major plot in the gospel is the conflict with "the Jews" who primarily represent the Jewish leaders. Jesus is the replacement for these leaders (he is the "good shepherd" for example).

4. Witness (Revelation and Response)

The Witness theme is one that bridges the two major groupings. Under Revelation, Jesus' mission is to witness to himself and the Father. The contrast to Jesus as true witness are the "Jews" who seek to thwart the mission of Jesus throughout the gospel.

Witness also belongs to Response because the theme is played out among those who witness the truth about Jesus: John the Baptist, disciples, Samaritan woman, blind man, and others. Ultimately those who follow Jesus are sent by him as witnesses to the world.

5. Believing (Response)

"Believing" is the primary term John uses to express responses to Jesus, but is actually only representative of many terms for responding to Jesus, such as seeing, knowing, following, remaining, etc. The Believing theme in John utilizes these terms with different levels of meaning from inauthentic believing to authentic believing (or seeing or knowing). This theme is concerned with the true nature of believing, not mere intellectual assent or mere emotional response.

6. Signs (Response)

The Signs theme is firmly tied to Believing in the gospel, but is a distinct theme primarily involving motifs of "signs" and "works." The miraculous signs, several of them numbered, serve the purpose of accentuating the identity of Jesus especially as life-giver. These few signs are only representative of Jesus' works. The Signs *theme*, though, is primarily about the response of people to the signs. As we will see, the responses to the signs are varied as well as illuminating for the nature of true believing (or not believing). Though the Signs theme is perhaps the most limited of the seven and closely related to Believing, yet because of the defined objective nature of the signs and their purpose, I treat the theme separately.

7. Destiny (Revelation and Response)

The Destiny theme regards the eschatological results of positive and negative responses to the love of God for the world, eternal life and judgment, respectively. Though God sent Jesus to save the world, the world largely rejects that love. John expresses this concept most clearly in 3:16–18 but certainly incorporates the theme throughout the gospel. Included in this theme is the ambiguous relation of God's sovereignty and the free will of humanity. In addition, Jesus himself has a destiny in the gospel, most notably played out in the motif of the "hour." Time itself is an important part of this theme.

MULTI-THEMATIC MOTIFS

These seven themes largely cover the major theological ideas in John's gospel. There are arguably other "themes" but usually these are actually motifs which fit under the umbrella of the themes indicated above. One example is the Paraclete/Holy Spirit. The Spirit is a motif which aligns with the multiple themes of Identity, Life, Witness and even Destiny. The themes focused on in this book are much wider in scope and observable in every major section of the gospel.

There is one infused motif that cuts across every theme—the cross. By infused I simply mean that the cross is always in view in the gospel and is arguably part of every theme, though not necessary an explicitly stated concept. In this sense the cross is not a motif proper, but is a profoundly guiding image that the careful reader can detect from the Prologue to the end of the gospel. At some point in each thematic essay, I will address how the cross plays a role in that particular theme.

The rest of the book includes two major parts and a short appendix. Part One systematically delves into each theme and the motifs which contribute to each theme throughout the text of John. The organization of each chapter varies, since John uniquely presents each theme according to its character and purposes. Each chapter, however, will have a section on the introduction of the theme in the Prologue, so that by the end of Part One, a full thematic analysis of the Prologue is available. Part Two is synthetic in nature: I examine three sections of John and show how the themes intertwine and interact with each other to create complexity and depth in John's theological portrait of Jesus.

So let's dive into the deep and satisfying waters of the Gospel of John and find untold treasure for our lives!

PART ONE

Thematic Essays

1

Identity

"WHO ARE YOU?" THE Jewish leaders ask Jesus in John 8:25. Their question is the most basic question reflected on in the Gospel of John. John's answer to the question is complex, but unified. Jesus is the very revelation of God: the divine Son, the Savior of the world, the hoped for Messiah of the Jews, the true Witness to God the Father. These fairly simple epithets are the essential elements of the first four themes: Identity, Life, Festival and Witness. Each theme embodies one complex of images related to the nature of Jesus as the revelation of God.

The Identity theme sets out the divine nature of Jesus Christ. From beginning to end this gospel is concerned to show where Jesus Christ comes from, whose authority he acts under, the scope of his nature and authority, and his destiny in returning to his place of origin. As such, the Identity theme infuses the gospel from start to finish.

Pilate asks Jesus a fundamental Identity question, "Where are you from?" (19:9). The readers of the gospel know the answer is "from heaven." A number of scholars have illustrated the coming of Jesus in the Gospel of John with a "V" indicating his coming from the Father (heaven) to earth and then his return. The gospel story takes place at the bottom point of the "V" at a moment in time, but the larger story is timeless with a "beginning" before creation and an "ending" in eternity forward. John seeks to show in the Identity theme that Jesus Christ on earth was the very picture of what he always was and always will be, God.

Identity encompasses a number of images and motifs which John may introduce only once, such as the *Logos*, or which he expands significantly, such as the Son motif. Identity motifs include preexistence, an extensive "Son" motif with various combinations, and the absolute "I am" sayings. As pointed out in the introduction, this theme and its associated motifs weave together with other themes and their associated motifs, creating an endless web of relationships and possibilities for meaningful observations. Of further note is the function of these Identity motifs in John's plan. Each instance of the Identity theme serves as a riddle for the reader (or hearer) to reflect on regarding the divine nature of Jesus and come to a decision concerning its meaning and the claim that is made on one's life. Every question in the text is also a question for the reader.

Because the Identity theme concerns Jesus' divine identity, the theme as outlined here does not include elements related to Jesus as Savior or as the Jewish Messiah. The Life and Festival themes will cover these topics. As will be evident with every theme, Identity, while focusing primarily on Jesus and the meta-theme of Revelation, also includes an aspect that relates it to the meta-theme of Response. When people encounter Jesus and respond to him, their identity changes, and their true origin in God is revealed.

LOGOS

"In the beginning was the Word, and the Word was with God, and the Word was God." These opening phrases of the so-called "Prologue" of John (1:1–18) introduce the Identity theme. "The Word" (1:1) who became flesh (1:14) and reveals God (1:18) is the dominant idea of these eighteen verses. The "Word" (Gk. *logos*, henceforth *Logos)* is the subject of the opening three phrases in John 1:1. This emphatic three-fold repetition makes an imprint on the rest of the gospel. The gospel is concerned preeminently with the revealing of the *Logos.* Though only used as a title in the Prologue (1:1–18) the *Logos* is clearly linked in an intimate and discreet way with the person of Jesus Christ (1:17). The Prologue is John's theological account of how this connection transpired, how the eternal *Logos* became the incarnate *Logos.*

John never defines the term *Logos,* but does associate *Logos* with God. The *Logos* existed with God in the beginning. For John, God and *Logos* always existed together. The relationship between the two is expressed as "the *Logos* was *with* God". "With" (Gk. *pros*) is not a static concept, but expresses the idea of "motion toward." *Logos* and God have a constant eternal movement toward each other. The third phrase in 1:1, "and the *Logos* was God," expresses even more clearly the divine character of the *Logos.* The NEB attempts to get at the meaning of the phrase with the expression "and what God was the Word was." The grammatical structure implies that the *Logos* is fully God, but not the totality of God. Neither was the *Logos* any less than God. In formulating the divine identity of the *Logos* this way, John lays the foundation for Trinitarian theology. This formulation also prevents modalistic thinking about God; in the Incarnation, God the Father and God the Son existed together, one did not become the other.

Why does John use the term *logos*? Likely because only this term allowed John to bring to expression his understanding of how God revealed himself in the Incarnation. The Greek term *logos* has an extremely wide range of meanings in ancient literature. The Liddell-Scott Lexicon lists nine major categories of meaning with numerous specific renderings including: account, saying, story, relation, ratio, explanation, reason(ing), a speech, and other types of verbal statements. In the Gospel of John the term *logos* often refers to a variety of statements or utterances, primarily those of Jesus. Only in the Prologue, however, does John use the term *logos* in a personal sense to refer to the manifestation of God, which is the active force in creation and ultimately the incarnation of God in Jesus Christ.

The use of this wide-ranging Greek term allows John to refer to both Hebrew and Greek conceptions. First, in using *logos* John draws from Genesis, where God speaks creation into existence, and the rest of the Hebrew scriptures, which refer to the word of the Lord (LXX, *logos kyriou)* to Abraham, Jacob, Moses or any of the prophets.

Besides drawing on the rich tradition of the speech of God in creation and to the prophets of Israel, John employs *logos* in an age where the Platonic, Stoic, and Hellenistic Jewish traditions have imbued the term with philosophical depth. It is impossible to know the extent to which John was aware of these traditions, but certainly the first generations of readers of the Gospel discerned these connections. The Stoics conceived of the *Logos* as the impersonal force of coherence that held the universe together. The Jewish philosopher Philo drew on Platonism and Jewish Wisdom traditions to conceive of the *Logos* as the active force of God in creation and humanity. Philo never conceived of the *Logos* as incarnated in a person, however. John makes this conception clear with the phrase, "and the *Logos* became flesh and dwelled among us" (1:14).

While John 1:1–2 sets out the relationship of the *Logos* to God, verse three introduces the scope of the divine authority of the *Logos*: "All things were made through him, and apart from him nothing was made which was made." Not only is the *Logos* identified with God, but a specific function of the *Logos* is creation. The *Logos* is the agent of creation. John is specifically alluding to the active speech of God in Genesis 1 and maybe to the wisdom traditions in Proverbs.[1] By the time John wrote the Prologue, several other Christian writers had formulated similar ideas about the role of Jesus Christ in creation (1 Cor 8:6; Col 1:16–17; Heb 1:2). John is the only one to use *logos*, though the author of Hebrews says it similarly: "in these last days, [God] has *spoken* to us in a Son" (Heb 1:2, italics mine). The *Logos* is the divine agency of the Godhead involved in creating all things and communicating to that very creation.

The succeeding verses of John's Prologue develop several characteristics of the *Logos*, primarily the *Logos* as light and life. These important images are part of the separate though related theme of Life, which I will take up in the next chapter.

The important transition point in the Prologue with regard to Identity occurs in 1:14: "And the Word (*Logos*) became flesh and dwelled among us and we beheld his glory, glory as of the only-begotten of the Father, full of grace and truth." We as readers do not yet know the full meaning of this verse. We do know that the *Logos* is now human like us. We also know the *Logos* is uniquely from the Father in the role of "only-begotten" (Gk. *monogenēs*).[2]

John goes on to specify who the *Logos* made flesh is as a particular human; in 1:17 he identifies the *Logos* with Jesus Christ. From this point on, the gospel writer intends that every word and act of the man Jesus are those of the divine *Logos*. This idea is confirmed in 1:18: "the only-begotten God who is in the bosom of the Father, has made him known."[3] One irony of the gospel is that the actors in the gospel must discover this identity for themselves.

The revealing of the *Logos* in these eighteen verses only commences the Identity theme. The *Logos* as a title does not appear again in John; instead the motifs of "preexistence," "the Son" and the phrase "I am," take over to definitively connect the person of Jesus Christ with the *Logos*.

---

1. Cf. Ps 33:6; Wis 9:1–2; Prov 8:22–31.

2. Most translations include the identification "Son." The term for Son (Gk. *huios*)is not present, only implied by context.

3. Note that some translations read "only-begotten Son." The earliest manuscripts read "God (Gk. *theos*)," but a large number of significant texts read "Son (Gk. *huios*)."

These motifs are actually present in the Prologue and continue as John tells the gospel story.

Finally, while John focuses primarily on the identity of the *Logos* in the Prologue, there is another pertinent observation. In 1:12–13, John speaks of those who have received the *Logos*. This notice properly belongs to the Believing theme. However, in that those who receive the Logos become "children of God" and are "born from God," we have an extension of the Identity theme. The identity of these people has changed from "born of the world" to "born of God." Throughout the gospel we will observe this change of identity as people place their trust in the incarnate *Logos*, Jesus Christ.

PRE-EXISTENCE

While is is fairly obvious from the Prologue that the *Logos* was preexistent as part of the Godhead, John goes on to connect this eternal state with the person of Jesus. The repetition of the concept makes pre-existence a sort of motif for the Identity theme.

John the Baptist is the character who introduces the concept with reference to Jesus. When "the Word became flesh," the Baptist proclaims, "This was the man of whom I spoke, one is coming after me who is now ahead of me, because he existed before me" (1:15). John the Baptist's statement indicates the pre-eminence of the incarnate *Logos* because of the pre-existence of that very *Logos*. The John the Baptist narrative of 1:18–34 continues this motif by repeating the same phrase in 1:30 after identifying Jesus as "the Lamb of God who takes away the sin of the world." The repetition of 1:15 in 1:30 connects the *Logos* of the Prologue to the man Jesus (as in 1:17), and continues the motif of pre-existence in the gospel.

The gospel goes on to make this motif explicit in a number of cases, though it usually occurs in conjunction with other Identity motifs. In the public ministry, Jesus refers to his pre-existence explicitly in 6:62 (along with the descent/ascent motif) and 8:58 (with the "I am" motif). In the prayer of John 17, Jesus prays, "Glorify me, Father, with your glory which I had with you before the world existed" (17:5), and later, "because you loved me before the foundation of the world" (17:24). Throughout the gospel, when Jesus speaks of his origin as "from above" or the like, the pre-existence motif is in play. The gospel clearly wants to portray the man Jesus as the embodiment of the pre-existent divine *Logos*. By the time Pilate asks Jesus, "Where are you from?" the reader knows the answer not only in terms of place, "from heaven," but also in terms of time, "from eternity."

SON

When Jesus speaks to the crowds in Jerusalem at the end of his public ministry and tells them he must "be lifted up," some in the crowd ask, "Who is this Son of Man?" (12:34). For the reader of the gospel the answer is fairly clear at this point. This "Son of Man" a.k.a. "Son of God" a.k.a. "only-begotten Son" a.k.a. "the Son" is Jesus, the divine *Logos* made flesh. This extensive "Son" motif is the dominant one for the Identity theme, with each variation being a sub-motif. Scholars differ over whether John has truly distinct ideas in mind for each variation. Ultimately, however, the "Son" in whatever variation is inarguably the divine manifestation of God in the *Logos* made flesh.

Son of God

In the baptism scene of John 1, John the Baptist makes the declaration: "I have seen and I have testified that this one is the Son of God" (1:34).[4] What the Baptist means by this bold declaration is yet to be determined; "Son of God" is certainly an Identity statement meant to add to what the reader already knows. "Son" in a variety of different phrases now becomes a key Identity motif throughout the gospel. The Baptist makes this remarkable identification because of what he witnessed in light of his own revelation from God, namely the alighting of the Spirit upon Jesus as the indication of the one who would baptize with the Holy Spirit. In what may be words of the Baptist or at least a commentary on his words, John 3:31–36 develops this understanding of the Son of God by pointing to Jesus origin from heaven (3:31), and to Jesus as the one sent from God who "speaks the words of God" and who has "the Spirit without measure" (3:34).

There is a second declaration of Jesus as Son of God later in John 1. After Jesus has surprised Nathaniel with his insight, Nathaniel declares, "You are the Son of God, you are the King of Israel." Unlike John the

---

4. There are two Greek NT manuscripts, one of them the Codex Sinaiticus, as well several Latin manuscripts, that have an alternative reading, "Chosen one of God," a reading that would seem to fit the progression of titles throughout John 1:29–51. The vast weight of manuscript evidence is for "Son of God."

Baptist's identification, Nathaniel is likely making a claim related to the royal status of Jesus rather than as equal to God.[5] This identification would more properly go with the Festival theme.

"Son of God" does not appear again in John until 3:18 (see below on "only-begotten"). There it is quite clear that the phrase should be understood as an identification of the Son of God in its full divine sense as in all subsequent uses (5:25; 11:4, 24; 20:21).

Descent and Ascent of the Son of Man

John adds additional perplexity to the "Son" motif when he includes Jesus' statement about the "Son of Man" in 1:51: "You will see the angels ascending and descending upon the Son of Man." "The Son of Man" is arguably part of a discreet motif of the Identity theme that involves a combination of three images: "descent," "ascent" and "the Son of Man." Since the key image includes "Son" and is closely related to "Son of God," I take up all these images here.

The gospel has already initiated a "descent" motif in the baptism scene. In 1:33, John the Baptist testified, "I saw the Spirit descending like a dove from heaven and it remained upon him," which led him to conclude: "he is the one who baptizes with the Holy Spirit." The motion of descent might be implied in the Prologue ("he was the true light coming into the world"), but in 1:33, the actual word "descend" (Gk. *katabainō*) occurs. "Descend" often appears with its opposite "ascend" (Gk. *anabainō*). In this instance, it is the Spirit that descends as an indicator that Jesus is the one designated by God to give the Holy Spirit. Until the post-resurrection appearances of Jesus, the only person in the gospel with the Spirit is Jesus (cf. 3:34b, 7:39). There is no clear Trinitarian theology expressed in John, but the implication for such a theology begins with the baptism scene.

"Descent" language takes on a much more important role as the gospel proceeds. John indicates this pattern in the gospel through the use of descent and ascent terminology. He goes on to emphasize that Jesus as the Son of Man is the one who has descended and who later will ascend. At the beginning of this chapter, I pointed out that there is a "V" shape to the gospel. The divine *Logos* comes from eternity to the world of humanity and ultimately returns to the Father. In so doing, the divine identity is emphasized.

5. Cf. the coronation pronouncement in Ps 2:7.

As noted earlier, the first clear instance of this motif related to the Identity of Jesus is in 1:51. At the end of a long passage related primarily to the Festival and Witness themes (1:35–51), Jesus responds to the faith of Nathaniel with "Truly, truly I say to you (plural), you will see heaven open and the angels of God ascending and descending upon the Son of Man." The statement arguably belongs with the Festival theme, since Jesus is drawing on the Old Testament story of Jacob's ladder.[6] But Jesus is actually making a statement about his Identity as the Son of Man who is the way to heaven; only the rest of the gospel, however, will explain what the statement means! In other words, we have a puzzle to be solved. For the purposes of the motif, we have our three important elements of descend, ascend and Son of Man in combination. Here it is the angels who ascend and descend *on* the Son of Man. But in the remainder of the gospel, it is the Son of Man who descends from heaven and ascends to heaven via the cross and resurrection.

The most important piece of this puzzle is the phrase "Son of Man." Students of the Synoptic Gospels (Matthew, Mark and Luke) are familiar with the term as Jesus' self-designation, taking the place of "I." This oft-used self-designation is especially noticeable in the passion predictions. But Jesus also refers to an apocalyptic "Son of Man" (drawing from Dan 7:13) as the one who will return with the angels of heaven and who will be seated at the right hand of God (cf. Matt 16:27; 19:28; 24:30; 25:31). Jesus connects these two uses at the trial before Caiaphas when asked if he was the Messiah: "I am," Jesus states, "and you will see the Son of Man seated at the right hand of power and coming with the clouds of heaven" (Mark 14:62; cf. Matt 26:64). In John, "Son of Man" moves even beyond the apocalyptic language of the Synoptic Gospels and designates the Son of Man as "from heaven" as well as going to heaven (3:13; 6:62). For John, "Son of Man" implies the divine status of Jesus, at least on par with "Son of God." Some scholars have argued it is the title for Jesus *par excellence*. When Jesus speaks of the Son of Man in John, however, it never loses its primary reference of "I."

Clues to this Identity puzzle begun in 1:51 come in 3:13–14. At the conclusion of his conversation with Nicodemus (with its own Identity motifs), Jesus states, "no one has ascended into heaven, except for the

---

6. As is always the case with John, motifs never stand alone, but occur in changing combinations with other motifs and even themes. The descent/ascent motif certainly qualifies.

one who has descended from heaven, the Son of Man." The statement is enigmatic at best. Its position comes directly after Jesus has lightly scolded Nicodemus for being obtuse in understanding "heavenly" matters. In 3:13 Jesus declares why. The only individual qualified to speak of heavenly things is the Son of Man who has descended from heaven. As I note in the analysis of 3:1–21 in Part 2, there were a number of claims by apocalyptic seers to have entered heaven and seen the mysteries of God. Jesus disparages these claims. The Son of Man is the only one to know these mysteries because he *is* from heaven.

Jesus continues that this Son of Man from heaven is also the one who will be "lifted up" (3:14). Later in the gospel, John tells us clearly that "lifted up" means Jesus' crucifixion on the cross, thus bringing eternal life to those who believe (12:32–33). "Lift up" (Gk. *hupsoō*) is not an exact synonym of "ascend," but the intent is the same. The ascent of Jesus back to the Father takes place via his lifting up on the cross; John also uses "glorification" of the Son of Man in 12:23 to express the same idea. This multi-image sub-motif of the "descent and ascent of the Son of Man" appears again in John 6 (see Part 2).

John supplements the "ascent and descent of the Son of Man" aspect of the Son motif with an uncommon but significant image, the contrast of "above" and "below". Despite Jesus' descent to the world, he still remains "from above." The idea first appears in Jesus' conversation with Nicodemus. Jesus tells him, "You must be born from above" (3:3, 7), and then makes a contrast between earthly things and heavenly things in 3:12. Toward the end of the chapter, John (or perhaps a continuation of the speech of John the Baptist) declares in reference to the Son: "The one who comes from above is above all; that which is from the earth speaks earthly things. The one coming from heaven is above all" (3:31). We see this stark contrast one other time in 8:23 during a contentious debate with the Jewish leaders, where Jesus says, "You are from below, I am from above; you are from this world, I am not from this world." To Pilate, Jesus responds in a similar vein, "my kingdom is not from this world" (18:36).

An additional element related to "ascent" appears with the language of "going" (Gk. *hupagō* or *poreuomai*) and related terms. Jesus is referring to his return to the Father. Jesus first uses the language in his conversation with the Jewish leaders in 7:33: "Still a little while I will be with you and [then] I am going to the one who sent me." This language confuses (and exasperates) the Jewish leaders, but Jesus continues to speak in this way (8:14, 21). Later, in the entirely different context of the farewell speeches of John 13–16, Jesus repeatedly prepares the disciples for his impending departure using the same language (John 13:33, 36; 14: 2–4, 12, 28; 16:5, 7, 10, 17, 28).

Just as John has identified Jesus with God in his preexistence, with the spacial images of descent, ascent, above and below, and return to the Father, John has identified Jesus' origin and home as with the Father in heaven. The identification "Son of Man" brings together his origin and his destiny to bring salvation to the world.

Only-begotten Son

The two most important statements regarding the Son of Man come in 3:13–14, where the Son of Man descends from heaven, and then is "lifted up" via the cross. Immediately following these images, the "Son" motif takes a new turn. In 3:16, John writes, "God . . . gave his only-begotten Son." This is John's third use of the term "only-begotten" (Gk. *monogenēs*). The other two instances came in the Prologue, once used alone in "the only-begotten from the Father" (1:14, which all translations render with "Son," even though "Son" is only implied), and once in the phrase "only-begotten God" in 1:18. A look at various translations reveals a number of slightly different renderings of *monogenēs*: "only-begotten," "one and only," and "only." While "only-begotten" is a perfectly good translation (and the one I use for clarity's sake throughout this book), "one and only" and "only" get to the idea that this Son is unique in comparison with any other "son of God." Because of the make-up of the word in Greek (*mono*—"only" + *genes*—"begotten"), some groups tend toward a type of Arianism that argues that the Son is created, not eternally existent with the Father. John is far from this view, not least in his use of "only-begotten God" in 1:18. This type of thinking comes from the so-called "root fallacy" that takes a word's meaning as the literal denotation of the parts of the words. Context must take precedence in light of the way the word was understood when John used it.

At this point, the "Son" motif develops quickly. In John 3:17 we read "God . . . sent the Son."[7] "The Son of Man" turned "only-begotten Son" now simply becomes, "the Son." From now on in the gospel "the

---

7. Most translations have "his Son" because the definite article implies the relationship introduced in 3:16. The NASB has "the Son."

Son" implies both "Son of Man" and "only-begotten Son." Then right on the heels of these co-identifications, John writes in 3:18, "The one not believing is judged already because he has not believed in *the only-begotten Son of God.*" Within the five verses from 3:14–18 John uses each of these "Son" designations for Jesus.

Father and Son

The next progression in the Son motif regards the familial relationship between God and his Son at the end of the same chapter. The Prologue already stated this relationship in 1:14 ("glory as of the only-begotten of the Father") and 1:18 ("the only-begotten God who is in the bosom of the Father has made Him known"). Up to this point in John, however, the term "Father" (Gk. *patēr*) has not occurred again. This situation changes at the end of chapter 3. After making the remarkable Identity (and Witness theme) statement that "the one whom God has sent speaks the words of God for he has given him the Spirit without measure" (3:34), John goes on to say, "the Father loves the Son and has given all things into his hands" (3:35). If the relation of the *Logos* to God in the Prologue (and in 3:34!) is one of a more rational relationship in terms of communication, John 3:35 shows the intense familial relation already implied in 1:14, but now with the verb "love" (Gk. *agapaō*) used to define the relationship. Furthermore, this "love" is characterized by the action of giving "all things into his hands." There is no practical distinction between what the Father does and the Son does, because of this familial intimacy. From the gospel's perspective, this premise indicates that whatever the Son does as the Word become flesh is a very picture of what the Father does.

The most focused section for the Father and Son motif of the Identity theme occurs in John 5:17–27. In these paragraphs John "throws down the gauntlet" for the Identity theme. The reader who has carefully considered the Identity thread to this point has no option but to make a decision on the truth of John's perspective that Jesus is truly the Son of God—and this is what John wants.

Directly following the healing of the lame man at the start of John 5, Jewish leaders attempt to prosecute the healed man because he carried his mat on the Sabbath. Upon the man's testimony, however, the leaders turn their sights on Jesus, "because he did these things on the Sabbath" (5:16). Jesus makes an astounding statement to these leaders: "My Father is working up to now and I also am working." Immediately the Jewish leaders attempt to put Jesus to death because "he called God his own Father, making himself equal to God."

Why would they make the leap from what Jesus said to equality with God? One of the current debates of the rabbis during that period concerned whether God did any work on the Sabbath or not. The basic conclusion was that God "worked" by giving life and judging in that births and deaths still occurred on the Sabbath. Jesus not only calls God, "Father," but claims to be doing the same Sabbath work as the Father!

It must be said that in Jesus' response to their outrage, he is actually downplaying their conclusion that he is making himself equal to God. Again and again he tells them that he does nothing unless the Father tells him. But in his attempt to downplay their accusation, he actually affirms his Identity as fully bound to the Father in a divine relationship. The statement of 3:35 is repeated again with a slight twist: "The Father loves the Son and shows him everything he does" (5:20).[8]

Further, the Father shows and gives over to the Son his two major ongoing tasks. First as the Father gives life, now the Son gives life. Second as the Father judges, so the Son judges. In other words, the Son acts in every way that the Father acts! The actions of giving life and judging are not just for the present, but also for the future (5:24–29). In this passage, John makes clear that Jesus' self-referent "I" of 5:17 is the same as "the Son" (19, 20, 21, 22, 23, 26), "the Son of God" (25), and "the Son of Man" (27).

In the remainder of the gospel, Father and Son language becomes normative for Jesus' references to God and himself, respectively. This language is especially evident in the interaction of Jesus and those who oppose him (cf. John 6, 8, 10). The status quo that John sets out in chapter 5 remains until the aftermath of the healing of the blind man (John 9). In the latter half of John 10, however, during Hanukkah, another argument breaks out between the Jewish leaders ("the Jews") and Jesus. They ask Jesus, "If you are the Christ, tell us plainly." Jesus responds in 10:25–30 with words combining six of the themes![9] Jesus invokes Father/Son

---

8. Instead of the Greek verb for love used in 3:35, *agapaō*, the verb *phileō* occurs. John uses the terms synonymously.

9. "I told you and you do not believe me (Believing). These works that I am doing in the name of my Father (Signs) testify concerning me (Witness). But you do not believe (Believing), because you are not from my sheep (Destiny). My sheep hear my voice and I know them and they follow me (Believing and Destiny), and I give eternal life to them

language as before, but in the final statement makes an astounding claim unlike any previous ones, "I and the Father are one." John's notice that the Jews took up stones to stone him is a key indicator of the implications of Jesus' words and they tell Jesus as much, "we are stoning you . . . because you who are a man make yourself God" (10:33). Later during Jesus' trial, they tell Pilate that "he ought to die, because he made himself out to be Son of God" (19:7).

I will only note briefly that the Father/Son relationship is on full display in the Farewell speeches to the disciples in John 13–17. To Philip, Jesus says, "He who has seen me has seen the Father," and proceeds to develop this contention in the following verses. John 15 and 17 also illustrate the relationship (see Part Two for John 17).

The "Son" motif is the heart of the Identity theme. When John states that "these things are written so you might believe that Jesus is . . . the Son of God" we have no doubt about what he means. Jesus as the Son is truly the divine Son, the "only-begotten God who is in the bosom of the Father."

"I AM"

Maybe the most provocative presentation of the Identity theme in John comes in the so-called absolute "I am" statements. The phrase "I am" (Gk. *egō eimi*) occurs in words of Jesus twenty-three times throughout the gospel. In ten of these, a distinctive predicate follows "I am," such as "I am the bread of life," or "I am the light of the world." These predicate uses of "I am" belong predominantly to the Life theme, since each has something to do with Jesus' role as life-giving savior. The other use causes debate however, because the phrase stands alone (or "absolute") without a predicate. In everyday usage this absolute *ego eimi* served as a simple identification statement, "I am he" or "I'm that person." The healed blind man in John 9:9 uses the phrase in exactly that way when asked by his neighbors if he was the blind man: he kept saying, "I am."

When we look at how Jesus uses the phrase, however, this simple self-identification is not so clear. Indeed, when we read the response of Jesus in 8:58, "Before Abraham was, I am," it is obvious that something

---

(Life) and they will never perish forever and no one will snatch them from my hand (Destiny). My Father who has given me all things (Identity) is greater and no one will snatch them from my Father's hands (Destiny). I and the Father are one (Identity)."

more is meant, especially since the listeners "took up stones to throw at him" (8:59).

The absolute use of "I am" strictly occurs at 6:20; 8:24, 28, 58; 13:19; 18:5 (twice), 8. In the first instance, Jesus has just appeared to his disciples walking on the water. In response to their fear, Jesus says, "I am; don't be afraid." Even if one argues for the rendering, "It's me, don't be afraid," the scene is indicative of a divine theophany.[10] In John 8, the frame for understanding Jesus' use of the phrase comes in 8:23 in which "I am" occurs: "You are from below, I am from above; you are from this world, I am not from this world." "I am" in 8:24 and 28 simply makes no sense as simple identification, but as Jesus' identification with the very nature of God.

The last instance of the absolute use occurs in the arrest scene of John 18. When Jesus asks the soldiers who they are looking for and they respond, "Jesus of Nazareth." Jesus identifies himself with the words "I am." This response seems straightforward—except that the soldiers fell back to the ground when Jesus spoke the words. This notice is arguably a very subtle use of the "I am" motif for the Identity theme, but in light of the previous uses, John likely wants to remind his readers that the divine Son of God is on the way to the hour of his crucifixion.

Though the "I am" statements with a predicate are different from the absolute uses in that they are focused on the Life theme (see the next chapter), the implication of the absolute "I am" statements with regard to Jesus' divine nature are still present, especially when one realizes that images such as Light and Shepherd are key images of God in the Old Testament. In fact, the "I am" statements with a predicate usually have several themes implied in theme including Identity, Life and often Festival and Witness. They embody the Revelation meta-theme perhaps more clearly and succinctly than any other construction.

THE CROSS

Whether explicit or implicit, the cross is a motif that belongs to each of the themes. Some observers have attempted to down-play the cross, saying that it is secondary to John's purpose of showing Jesus as the divine revealer of God. What is ignored, however, is that Jesus' revelation of the Father takes place in the cross. The cross, in fact, is the place where Jesus

10. See Gen 15:1; 26:24; and especially Isa 41:10.

is "glorified." The cross is where Jesus as God is most evident. When John writes in the Prologue, "we beheld his glory, glory as of the only-begotten of the Father" he may have in mind Jesus life, but more so he has in mind Jesus' glory as revealed on the cross.

With regard to the Identity theme, there are at least two places in John that more explicitly connect the cross to Jesus' identity as divine. First is an incident at the close of Jesus' public ministry in John 12. Jesus is teaching in the temple and some Greeks come looking for Jesus. Upon hearing of this inquiry, Jesus says, "The hour has come for the Son of Man to be glorified" (12:23). That Jesus means the cross as the locale of glorification is evident in 12:24: "truly, truly I say to you, unless a grain of wheat falls to the earth and dies, it remains alone; but if it dies, it bears much fruit." That glorification on the cross is indicative of his divine Identity comes with the title, Son of Man, and also with the affirmation from God in response to Jesus request, "Father, glorify your name" that "I have glorified it and I will glorify it again" (12:28). In the cross, the true glory of God in Jesus Christ shows forth.

The passion narrative illustrates the Identity theme on several accounts. As pointed out in the "I am" motif, John subtly points to Jesus' identity when at the arrest the soldiers say they are seeking Jesus of Nazareth, Jesus says "I am" and the soldiers fall to the ground. In relation to the actual crucifixion, John presents Jesus' identity as the primary reason the Jewish leaders wanted him crucified. John portrays Pilate as very reluctant, but the Jewish leaders state that "we have a law and according to that law, he ought to die, because he made himself the Son of God." From their perspective they want Jesus dead because they believe he was indeed making this claim. There is no doubt that John believes the claim to be absolutely true!

Finally, when Jesus speaks the words, "It is finished," on the cross, the Father-Son relationship is in view. The Son came to complete all that the Father wanted him to do. On the cross, that work was accomplished. On the cross, the Word made flesh revealed the glory of the only-begotten of the Father.

CONCLUSION

Throughout the last two millennia there have been some who have sought to downplay the notion of Jesus as fully God. Some have even used John in this endeavor, arguing that John 1:1c should be translated "the Word was *a god*." Though possible, an understanding of ancient Greek makes this translation highly unlikely. But more than this linguistic argument, an understanding of the Identity theme in John shows definitively that John does not think that translation possible. Through the various motifs of the Identity theme, John's view is clear: Jesus Christ is fully God.

2

Life

"**D**o you wish to be well?" This question is not just one that Jesus' asks the lame man in John 5, but one that John asks the reader. For John the only one who can make a person "well" is Jesus. The Life theme points to Jesus Christ as the life-giving Savior of the world. The name of the theme comes from the prominence of the term "life" (Gk. *zōē*), a word which occurs 36 times in John and with its related verb "to live" over 50 times. This theme represents the saving purpose of the incarnation (3:15,16; 20:21). The result of this saving purpose, "eternal life," flows from the One who is life (1:4; 3:19–21; 5:26, 6:33 et al.). Although the terms "save," "salvation," and "savior" are rare in John (3:17, 4:22, 42; 5:34; 10:9; 11:12; 12:27, 47), the concept of salvation (or perhaps, Jesus as Savior) is essentially synonymous with life. But more than just these terms characterize the Life theme; Life also includes a number of images/motifs that are symbolic of, or related to, the life in and given through Jesus Christ, including light, bread, water, wine, resurrection, and to some extent, Spirit. All of the "I am" statements with a predicate ("I am the light of the world;" "I am the good shepherd;" etc.) belong with this theme. As with every theme, John includes dualistic counter-motifs. The Life theme is set in relief by the opposite motifs of darkness, night, death and related terms. John's dualism is very evident in this theme.

The Life theme enters early in the Prologue and never stays far from the surface throughout the gospel. Life appears especially prominent in the public ministry of Jesus in the first 12 chapters, though the depth of life for the believer is pronounced in chapters 13–17. All of Jesus' miracles (or "signs") in the gospel point to Jesus as life. Most of them actually show the life-giving character of Jesus. The healing of the blind man in John 9, for example, connects Jesus' life-giving power with light, one of the prominent motifs of this theme.

Images included in the Life theme, such as life and light, water and food, are universal concepts common to all peoples, languages and cultures. In whatever language they occur these concepts point to fundamental elements of our existence and survival as creatures on this planet. Life would be impossible without food, water and light. The lack of these necessities results in death. John uses these fundamental images to explore the purpose and outcome of the incarnation, salvation for the world. John draws on a rich background of OT language that focuses on God as the source and giver of life.

John rarely uses these images in a literal sense, except for when he uses the literary device of misunderstanding, where the person conversing with Jesus takes what Jesus says literally instead of symbolically (e.g., "new birth" as actual birth, "living water" as actual water, "bread from heaven" as manna). Indeed the very reason for highlighting the misunderstandings is to point to the deeper spiritual significance of the images. Thus, the new birth (actually "born again" or "born from above") is a birth into eternal life; living water is the ever-flowing life that comes from Jesus Christ; bread from heaven/bread of life is that spiritual food of and from Christ; light (of the world) is the God-given ability to see spiritual realities.

The Life theme is so infused into every part of the gospel, it is difficult to trace a progression. There is virtually no development, but simply the almost ubiquitous presence of the theme throughout the gospel. In the remainder of the chapter, then, I will illustrate its presence in selected sections beginning with the introduction of the theme in the Prologue and then its use in the miraculous "signs," several dialogues and in the specialized form of the predicated "I am" statements. As a result, the student will have a clear path to recognize the theme of Life throughout the gospel.

"IN HIM WAS LIFE"

John introduces the Life theme in the first section of the Prologue (1:1–18): "that which came to be in him was *life* and the *life* was the *light* of men (1:4)." "Him" in this instance is the *Logos*, who was with God, who was God, and through whom all things were created (1:1–3). The *Logos* not only created all things, but the ongoing acts of the *Logos* brought life. This life is not just physical life but what will later be called "eternal" life. A small change is made with the second mention of life in that the definite article is added: "and *the* life was the light of men." Life is a concept in the first phrase ("in him was life"), but in the second phrase life becomes a personal entity equated to the *Logos*, which is then equated with light. Life is both an inherent characteristic of the *Logos* and the *Logos* is the source of life for all creation. "The life" and "the light" are phrases Jesus uses of himself later in the gospel (8:12; 9:5; 11:10; 12:46; 14:6), where their implications become more explicit. Here we only have a taste of what is to come.

The focus of the light is humankind, thus John does not intend physical light, but spiritual light. This observation is necessary because the next phrase introduces the counter-motif of darkness: "The light shines in the darkness and the darkness did not overcome it" (1:5). "Light" in the next several verses makes it immediately clear that light and darkness are images with a deeper level of meaning beyond the physical. With the term "darkness" John introduces the first dualistic antithesis in the gospel, light versus darkness. John does not explain darkness here, though he will explore its pervasiveness as a spiritual reality later in chapter 3. He accepts darkness as a reality, but draws attention to its inability to overcome the light.

John proceeds with this theme by clarifying the singular equation of the light with the *Logos* and not any created person. John the Baptist was sent from God, but was not *the* light; he was only a witness to the light so that others might believe in this light (1:6–8).

In contrast to John as witness to the light, "the true light, which enlightens all people, was coming into the world" (1:9). This true light is the *Logos*. As discussed in the previous chapter, the *Logos* is characterized in a very similar way to the figure of Wisdom in the Old Testament (see Proverbs 8). In the apocryphal Wisdom of Solomon, the figure of Wisdom is directly connected with light. Scholars debate whether the *Logos* as light in 1:9 is pre-existent or incarnate; is John speaking of the *Logos* in the Old Testament period or the life of Jesus among men, or both?[1] If one accepts that the life of Jesus was in concert with his pre-existence, both are likely intended. The light of the *Logos* in the world of men before the incarnation and the "light of the world" in the incarnation are the same in their action and the result. This observation leads to

1. See the perceptive treatment by Ashton, "The Transformation of Wisdom."

a two-layered understanding of John 1:10–11, "He was in the world and the world came about through him, but the world did not know him. He came to his own place and his own people did not accept him." Just as Israel rejected the light in the Old Testament period, so also the majority of Jews rejected Jesus, though in both periods some responded.

In any case, the emphasis that John places on the light here is two-fold. First, the *Logos* is the *true* light, rendering other claims to being the light as false. Second, the light continues to shine. The particular tense structure in Greek lends a strong on-going sense to the shining of the light and the coming of the light, in spite of any ignorance or rejection on the part of humanity.

The result of this shining light for humanity is new life, in particular "authority to be children of God" for those who receive the light. In verses 12 and 13, we have the introduction of another image of this theme, birthing from God, and thus the concept of new spiritual life. John makes the contrast with the physical very explicit: "who were born, not of blood or of the will of the flesh or of the will of man, but of God." This image of new birth is also in the conversation with Nicodemus in chapter 3, and alluded to at other points in the gospel.

Whatever the nature of the *Logos* as Life previous to 1:1–13 (as preexistent and/or incarnate), in 1:14 the *Logos* definitively takes on life as a human: "the Word became flesh and lived (dwelt) among us." From the viewpoint of John and those who witnessed (and believed) in the incarnate *Logos*, they saw him as shining forth the light of the Father: "and we saw his glory, the glory as the Father's only son, full of grace and truth." John is drawing here on the rich OT image of the glory of God often manifested in light. Though the term grace (Gk. *charis*) is only used here and in 1:16–17 in the entire gospel, it is an additional feature of the theme in that the grace or gift that Jesus brings is salvation. While John treats the law as a gift of God, it is grace in Jesus Christ that brings life.

The Prologue vigorously introduces the Life theme. The remainder of the gospel reiterates the theme in various ways and combines it with other themes to produce an infinitely rich picture of salvation in Christ.

LIFE AND THE SIGNS

John refers to the miraculous actions of Jesus in the Gospel of John as "signs," though an event such as the temple cleansing in chapter 2 also functions as a sign pointing to Jesus. Nonetheless, John uses the miraculous signs primarily to show how Jesus gives life or to lead to discussions on Jesus as the life-giver. Although the Signs theme (see chapter 6) is dependent on the miraculous signs, the Signs theme is *not* synonymous with the signs. Instead, the signs themselves are largely concerned with the other themes, the primary one of which is Life.

For example, at the wedding in Cana, Jesus' miracle provides a symbol of abundant life to the wedding by changing the water to wine. Jesus literally brings life to the wedding by providing honor to the wedding couple. I will look again at this passage in the Festival theme chapter. The images of water and wine later become quite significant for the Life theme in John 4 and 15. At the end of this miracle, however, John gives an interpretive framework in verse 11: "Jesus performed this first sign in Cana of Galilee and he revealed his glory." This comment contains the first use of "sign" (Gk. *sēmeia*) in John. By pointing out that the disciples beheld Jesus' glory, John is indicating that there is more to the miracle than a miraculous event; it is a "sign" that points to the significance of the one performing the miracle. The interpretive frame provided in 2:11 is the Signs theme proper. The miracle itself is primarily related to the Life and Festival themes.

The second and third miraculous signs occur consecutively in John 4:46–5:8, though the chapter divisions create the illusion that they should be treated entirely separately. Both of the miracles are healing miracles and both use repetition to highlight the Life theme.

In the recounting of the healing of the royal official's son in 4:46–54, the contrast between "live" and "die" is repeated with the emphasis on "live." The miracle story begins in 4:46 by recalling the water to wine miracle "where he made the water wine." Jesus has already shown himself as a life-giver before this miracle is told. The official asks Jesus to "come and *heal* his son, for he was about to *die*." After Jesus tested the official regarding his belief, the man implores, "come before my son *dies*." Jesus responds, "Go, your son *lives*." The next verses show repetition with "Your child *lives*" and "Your son *lives*." But the physical life that Jesus brings here leads to a deeper level of life, because the official "and his whole house believed." The sign points to Jesus as the life-giver who brings physical and eternal life. John once again connects this sign to the first by noting that the event was the second sign Jesus did when he came from Judea to Galilee. In writing this account John weaves together the themes of Life, Believing, and Signs, in a way that points to who Jesus is and what the ideal response to his identity as life-giver is.

John follows up the second miracle in Cana with one in Jerusalem during "a feast of the Jews," likely Sabbath (5:1). The miracle takes place at the five-porticoed pool of Bethesda. Here Jesus makes a lame man "well." Consonant with the previous miracle where "live" is repeated three times, in this one "well" (Gk. *hygiēs*) is repeated five times (5:6, 9, 11, 14, 15; six times if 7:23 is included). In addition, John refers to the lame man as "the one who was healed" in 5:10, and Jesus is called "the one who healed him" in 5:13. The emphasis of the miracle itself then is on Jesus' ability to make well.

Though significant for the Life theme on its own, the emphasis on Jesus' ability to heal or make well is simply the entree for the discussion to follow with the Jewish leaders on the prerogatives of Jesus as the emissary of the Father to "raise the dead" and "give life." Language of the Life theme is prominent in 5:21–27 with "raise the dead," "make alive," "eternal life," "pass from death to life," "those hearing will live," and "the resurrection of life." This language of life for those who believe (Believing language is also prevalent) comes from the Father and the Son who both "have life in [themselves]" (5:26).

The pattern of a miraculous sign showing Jesus as a giver of life followed by an extended dialogue or other expansion which develops the Life theme (as well as others) is evident in three other signs: the Feeding of the 5000, the healing of the blind man and the raising of Lazarus. I will look more carefully at these passages below as we consider several particular images of Life.

"I AM THE . . ."

Before looking at the particular images John uses to give richness to the Life theme, I want to point out one other primary vehicle for the expression of the theme in addition to the miraculous signs, namely, the "I am" statements followed with a predicate. In the previous chapter, we observed that the "I am" statements in John are of two types. The first is the absolute use of "I am" (Gk. *egō eimi*) which has no predicate nominative. The absolute use of the phrase is indicative of the identity of Jesus with regard to his divine origin and call (Identity theme). The most common construction, however, is the predicated "I am." In these cases, "I am" is followed by a predicate nominative consisting of a noun, a series of nouns, or a noun phrase, that serves to attribute to Jesus some life-giving image or function. These statements (and their variants) are well-known: "I am the bread of life," "I am the light of the world," "I am the gate," "I am the good shepherd," "I am the resurrection and the life," "I am the way, the truth, and the life," "I am the true vine." What is remarkable is that each predicate expresses an image related to the Life theme. It is worth pointing out, however, that these "I am" statements often connect with other themes, especially the other Revelation themes of Identity, Festival and Witness. For example, the images imbedded in "I am the Bread of Life" and "I am the Good Shepherd" have deep connections with the Old Testament as part of the Festival theme.

One notable aspect of each statement regards the use of the Greek article (Gk. *ho*, usually rendered as "the" in English) in each. Every predicate nominative in these "I am" constructions has the Greek article. While students of Greek will readily remember that the article is very complex and malleable in its uses, in these instances, the article is the most specific of all uses: the "monadic" article. The monadic article points to the noun as "one of a kind," or "unique." Jesus is not the *well-known* bread of life or the light of the world *par excellence*. No, he is the *only* gate, the *only* good shepherd, the *only* way, truth and life. The statements present Jesus as the one and only giver of Life, over against all others who would make such a claim. In the next sections of this chapter, we will look at most of these statements as they occur as part of particular motif complexes.

THE NECESSITIES OF LIFE

Food and water—without them we die. Human life and indeed all of physical life is predicated on the maintaining of a stable supply of food and water. John uses these fundamental images as motifs of the Life theme.

The water motif weaves in an out of the gospel, beginning with the baptism of John to the water to wine miracle, to "born of water and Spirit" in chapter 3 (as well as the notice—and dispute—about baptism in 3:23–26, cf. also 4:1), the woman at the well in chapter 4, the lame man at the Pool of Bethesda in 5, the cry of Jesus at Tabernacles in 7:38, the washing of the blind man at the Pool of Siloam in 9, the washing of the disciples feet in 13, and, not least, the notice of blood and water from Jesus' side in chapter 19. All are part of the Life theme.

The motif is particularly prominent in chapter 4. In all but the phrase itself, Jesus says, "I am the living water." When Jesus meets the Samaritan woman and asks "give me a drink" (4:7) and the woman responds in surprise that a Jewish man has made a request of her, Jesus responds, "if you knew the gift of God and who it is who says to you, Give me a drink, you would have asked him and he would have given you living water" (4:10). John writes with the literary technique of misunderstanding to contrast the literal sense that the woman takes and the spiritual sense that Jesus intends. The woman understands these words of Jesus as referring to spring-fed water, often referred to as "living water." In contrast, Jesus intends the words to refer to himself: "Everyone who drinks of this water which I give him will never thirst again, but the water which I give him will become in him a spring of water welling up to eternal life" (4:14). Jesus as the living water brings eternal life to those who drink of it. This section binds together the Life theme with the Believing theme (the verb "drink"), the Festival theme (Jesus as "greater than Jacob" and other elements), and the Destiny theme ("never thirst," "eternal life").

The images of food and particularly bread occur in several places in John. In the interlude to the story of the Samaritan woman, the disciples wonder where Jesus had gotten food and he responds: "I have food to eat that you don't know about . . . My food is to do the will of the one who sent me and to complete his work" (4:32, 33). In that short response, we already detect a symbolic meaning to food, although in that particular instance Jesus is mainly referring to the Witness theme. Jesus eats two meals with his disciples, one in chapter 13 and one in chapter 21. But in 13:26–27, we have a negative instance of the theme in that the dipping of the morsel indicates Judas as betrayer! In chapter 21, John makes notice of the great catch of fish and the subsequent breakfast on the shore. The catch of fish may point to the successful mission of the disciples in the world, though this interpretation is only one of many possible ones. The meal, however, with its notice of Jesus giving the bread and the fish to them, recalls the entire narrative of chapter 6.

In John 6, the author prominently displays the Life theme through the food/bread motif made apparent in the miracle (sign) of the feeding of the 5000 and the subsequent "Bread of Life" discourse. The sign itself in 6:5–15 follows the typical pattern of a nature miracle story as one might see in the Synoptic Gospels. This miracle is in fact the only one that appears in all four gospels (even Jesus' walking on the water does not appear in Luke). Miracle stories normally have a setting, a need, usually some sort of faith expressed, an action of Jesus, the miracle itself, and responses to the miracle. And indeed all of these elements are present in this story, though in some surprising ways that show Jesus as Life.

Jesus is the guiding force for the entire story. He notices the need for food and asks, "From where should we buy bread to feed these people?"(6:5). John immediately clues the reader that this question was essentially rhetorical in nature intended to get the disciples to think, for "[Jesus] himself knew what he was going to do" (6:6). The preface for this miracle (and "sign") indicates that what will happen is more about Jesus as the doer of the miracle than the miracle itself.

The next three verses (6:7–9) show the disciples' meager responses to Jesus along physical lines, first an expression of impossibility from Philip and then a miniscule presentation of food from a small boy with another doubtful question, "but what good is this for all these people?" If there is any faith expressed here it is barely perceptible. In this respect, this miracle is like the previous one in 5:2–9 where the lame man initially expresses no faith at all until he follows Jesus' command to get up.

Jesus is the one who supplies the faith; he directs the people into groups; he takes the bread; he gives thanks; he gives the bread and fish out. And he directs that the leftovers be gathered, "so that nothing might be lost" (6:12). This last statement could be an instance of "waste not-want not" but more likely is intended to evoke a question about the symbolism of the miracle. The verb "lost" (Gk. *apollymi*) appears previously in 3:16 and again in 6:27, 39 and later in John for the "perishing" of people (Destiny theme). This miracle is not simply about meeting the physical life needs of the people present, but more about the one who did the miracle, the giver of Life.

The story ends with an apparent response of faith from the crowd: "they began to say, 'This is indeed the Prophet who is to come into the world'" (6:14). This "prophet" is likely the expected prophet-like-Moses since it is clear from later in chapter 6 that the people likened the miracle to the giving of manna in the wilderness (see Festival theme). But the crowd misunderstood that the miracle was a sign pointing to the Life-giver; instead they saw Jesus as some political redeemer figure—"Jesus knew that they were about to come and seize him to make him king" (6:15)—whom they could follow in a revolution against Rome.

The true intent of the sign (and the misunderstanding of the crowd) becomes apparent in the conversation that ensues later in Capernaum. Jesus presents himself there as the true bread from heaven. There he states, "I am the bread of life." I will take up a detailed thematic study of this discourse in Part Two.

LIGHT AND DARKNESS

I have already shown how light and life are closely connected in the Prologue of John. Light is an archetypal image in all cultures and certainly for John's. The original word from God in Genesis 1, "And God said, let there be light," is foundational for this archetypal image throughout the Old and New Testaments.

The opposite image of darkness is also present in Genesis 1 and in the Gospel of John. As the gospel proceeds, light and darkness become important motifs of the Life theme. Perhaps the light-darkness contrast is the most starkly dualistic element in the gospel. The contrast between physical light and darkness (the absence of light) leads to symbolic contrasts in every human society, such as good and evil. The gospel certainly makes this good-evil contrast apparent, but also connects light with its life-giving properties. Without light, life does not exist, without light nothing grows, without light no one can see to carry out daily activities necessary to life. In John, Jesus is "the Light of the world."

Light and darkness as purely physical realities do occur in John such as when Nicodemus comes to Jesus at night in 3:2, or when the storm on the sea comes when it was already dark in 6:17. Others include a contrast between day and night in 11:9–10, or the notice "it was night" in 13:30, or that "it was still dark" when Mary Magdalene came to the tomb in 20:1. Even though these are literal instances, there is the sense that John is implying a deeper meaning. The abutment of "it was night" soon after the notice that Satan had entered Judas and that Judas had left to betray Jesus is without a doubt a *double entendre* referring to physical and spiritual night. Maybe John is also making a comment about the spiritual state of Nicodemus in 3:2.

Light and darkness as symbolic images are much more prominent, especially in John 3, 8 and 9. In 3:19–21, which I will take up as part of a thematic analysis in Part Two, John contrasts the "light coming into the world" with the observation that "people loved the darkness rather than the light." Those doing evil "hate the light" and those doing the truth "come to the light." John is melding spiritual light and darkness with good and evil as moral counterparts.

In John 8 during the festival of Booths (also referred to as Tabernacles), which featured a prominent light ceremony, Jesus proclaims, "I am the Light of the world; one who follows me will never walk in darkness, but will have the light of life" (8:12). Outside of the Prologue, this declaration is the most straightforward coupling of light to life. The two sentences together show a remarkably tight thematic integration of Identity ("I am"), Life ("the light of the world"), Festival (during Booths) Believing ("the one who follows me") and Destiny ("will never walk in darkness [i.e. judgment] but have the light of life [i.e. eternal life"). As such, this statement is one of the key gospel summaries that John has scattered throughout his gospel (see Appendix: The Gospel Summaries in John).

John 9 is the high point of the light-darkness motif in John as part of the Life theme. John crafts another unit that begins with a sign and then develops the physical aspects of the sign as symbolic images in the ensuing narrative. The sign and its dramatic continuation joins together the physical contrast of blindness and sight with night and day as well as the ethical contrast of sin and absence of sin (or godliness, a term that appears in v. 31).

The sign involves a man born blind from birth. The opening verses introduce all three contrasts noted above. Immediately in the aftermath of a heated debate during the festival of Booths in chapter 8, John introduces a man as "blind from birth" (9:1). The disciples ask what was likely a common question of the time, "Who sinned, this man or his parents?" (9:2). From the beginning of the chapter then, an ethical component is present which develops later on between the healed blind man and the Pharisees. The response of Jesus sets out the symbolic framework for the coming story: "Neither this man sinned, nor his parents, but (this happened) so that the work of God might be revealed in him. We must carry out the works of the one who sent me while it is day. Night is coming, when no one is able to work. While I am in the world, I am the light of the world" (9:3–5). The fact that Jesus and his disciples are facing a blind man, makes Jesus' claim not just a symbolic claim related to bringing God's life and truth to the world, but a practical claim with relation to the miracle that takes place in the next two verses (9:6–7). The result is that the blind man now sees the light.

A series of dramatic interactions make up the rest of the chapter, but Jesus only appears in the final two scenes. Instead, the now-seeing-blind-man is the key character. The important scenes for the light and darkness motif are those involving the Pharisees who interrogate the man because Jesus healed him on the Sabbath. The healed man testifies again and again that Jesus opened his eyes (9:15, 25, 30, 32). The Witness and Believing themes are quite prominent as the man grows in his faith and the Pharisees summarily reject his testimony over and over in unbelief. What is amazing is that despite the man's clear and compelling witness to the miracle, the Pharisees refuse to acknowledge that Jesus could have done the act because they deemed him a sinner for breaking the Sabbath. In response the man testifies, "we know that God doesn't listen to sinners, but if anyone is godly and does his will, God hears him. It's never been heard that anyone has opened the eyes of a person born blind. Unless God were with him, he would be unable to do anything" (9:31–33). John reminds us here of the initial conversation in 9:2–3 about who sinned. Not only is Jesus not a "sinner" but he also carries out the work of God that results in a life-giving act.

Ultimately the man comes to full faith in Jesus and worships him (9:35–38). When Jesus asks, "Do you believe in the Son of man" and the man responds, "Who is he that I might believe in him," Jesus says, "You have *seen* him and he is the one speaking to you." In conveying these words, John has made a small but significant change. All through chapter 9, John has used the verb for "see" which is common for physical sight, Gk. *blepō*. But here in 9:37, Jesus uses the other common word for "see," Gk. *oraō*. This latter Believing theme term is rarely used for simple sight, but rather for perception. John makes this distinction in almost every occurrence throughout the gospel.[2] Jesus who had already become the physical light for the man has now brought spiritual light to him. Jesus is "the Light of the world."

Jesus has a provocative word for the Pharisees in 9:39–41 that continues the imagery of blindness and sight, but the images are now connected to the Destiny theme. I will take up this short passage in the Destiny chapter.

---

2. Compare *blepō* in John 1:29; 5:19; 9:7, 15, 19, 21, 25, 39, 41; 11:9; 13:22; 20:1, 5; 21:9, 20; with *oraō* in John 1:18, 34, 39, 50–51; 3:11, 32, 36; 4:45; 5:37; 6:36, 46; 8:38, 57; 9:37; 11:40; 14:7, 9; 15:24; 16:16–17, 19, 22; 19:35, 37; 20:18, 25, 29.

One other image is worth noting as part of the light and darkness motifs. Earlier I briefly spoke of the interpretive comment that John makes about the water to wine miracle by calling the miracle a "sign." Another important element of that comment is a term not used since the Prologue, "glory" (Gk. *doxa*), which points to Jesus as the visible image of God in the world and has connotations of the *shekinah* of God in the Old Testament.

The term *doxa* has the basic idea of "reputation" or "honor" (see John 5:41, 44; 7:18; 8:50 et al.). The related verb *doxazō* encodes the idea of "to give repute" and thus to praise or honor or extol (e.g. John 8:54; 12:28; 14:13). The words have a variety of nuances in John, but when Jesus uses it later regarding himself or the Father, the terms have to to with the manifestation of the life-giving character of God in the world. Specifically the crucifixion indicates the life-giving character of God's glory in Jesus. When John says in 7:39 "but Jesus was not yet glorified," he is referring to the cross. This symbolic use of "glorify" occurs several times (12:16, 23; 13:31), but in cases such as the first sign we see that all of Jesus' life was intended to bring glory to God and likewise for the Father to show his glory in the son (see especially John 17).

DEATH AND RESURRECTION

Further images of the Life theme are resurrection and its opposite death. As eschatological outcomes for people this contrasting pair belongs with the Destiny theme. But John also sets resurrection as a key image of the Life theme in the Lazarus story of John 11, where Jesus tells Martha, "I am the Resurrection and the Life." Indeed John uses the Lazarus story to develop the Life theme in particular, though all of the themes are present at points. The physical raising of Lazarus from the dead is an image for the eternal life that Jesus gives to those who believe in him.

This miracle story is unique among all those in the gospels, even as a "sign" in John. There is a certain conciseness in most miracle stories, which normally include only essential features. If there is dialogue, that dialogue is quite focused. The other miracles in John consist of at most eleven verses (6:5–15). The account of the raising of Lazarus comprises forty-six verses at minimum, or fifty-three if you include all of the responses! The generic features of setting, need, request, faith expression, miracle and responses are all present, but John narrates each one to a far greater degree than is typical. This story also has unique qualities as one of the "signs" in John. Typically, the miraculous sign initiates a subsequent section that symbolically develops the sign (as seen in John 5, 6 and 9). In this instance, however, the symbolic development takes place as part of the miracle story itself. The actual miracle does not occur until the end of the passage in 11:43–44. Everything that occurs before this point builds up to the miracle. The way John narrates the episode shows that his primary concern regards Jesus as "the Resurrection and the Life."

The setting and need take up a quarter of the chapter (11:1–16). Jesus is across the Jordan with his disciples (10:40–42) and Mary, Martha and Lazarus are in Bethany near Jerusalem. We learn that Lazarus is sick and ultimately dies, facts repeated in various ways at least nine times. If one thing is not in question here, it is that Lazarus is dead! We also learn that Lazarus, Martha, and Mary are very dear to Jesus (he "loved" them). Jesus delays any action, however, "for the glory of God, so that the Son of God might be glorified through [the sickness]" (11:4). Since this incident is the precipitating factor for the passion in John, Jesus is ultimately "glorified" by the event as it leads to his crucifixion.

The request section of the miracle is where John delves intently into the Life theme. Upon Jesus' arrival, Martha tells Jesus, "Lord, if you had been here, my brother would not have died, but now I know that whatever you ask God, God will give to you" (11:20–21). Martha knows from prior experience that Jesus was capable of making someone well who was sick (see 11:37); her subsequent statement shows that her faith does not extend to bringing Lazarus back to physical life. When Jesus states, "Your brother will be raised," Martha responds, "I know he will be raised in the resurrection at the last day" (11:23–24). Martha is quite certain that Lazarus' faith will result in eschatological healing. Despite her limited response, Jesus affirms her certainty of future resurrection in a vital statement of the Life theme: "I am the resurrection and the life, the one who believes in me, though he dies, will live and everyone who lives and believes in me will never die forever" (11:25–26). This statement of Jesus is another concise, tightly integrated thematic statement of the gospel message in John akin to 3:16, 6:35, 40, and 8:12. This one includes Identity, Life, Believing and Destiny themes. Jesus himself embodies life and gives life to all who believe. As a response of faith to Jesus' question, "Do you believe this," Martha confesses, "Yes, Lord, I believe that you are the Christ, the Son of God who is coming into the world" (11:27).

The subsequent scene between Jesus and Mary serves primarily to build the narrative suspense between the finality of Lazarus' death and the (im)possibility of Jesus bringing him back from the dead. Mary repeats Martha, "Lord, if you had been here, my brother would not have died" (11:32). The crowd adds to the tension, "Was this man who opened the eyes of a blind man not able to keep this man from dying?" (11:37). John has developed another case of misunderstanding with a deep sense of irony. Jesus is concerned that "eternal life" for the world is the most important outcome of his action. Those present are focused more on the inability of Jesus to have made Lazarus physically well.

Nonetheless, Jesus goes ahead to perform the most audacious of his signs. He tells Martha, "Didn't I say to you, if you believe, you will see the glory of God?" and he then prays to the Father, "so [the crowd] might believe that you sent me" (11:40–41). When Lazarus emerges from the tomb, Jesus speaks words that are at the same time physical and deeply symbolic of Life: "Loose him and let him go."

SPIRIT

I indicated earlier in the introductory chapter that some motifs fit with multiple themes depending on how John situates that motif. The motif of the Spirit is the prime example. The Spirit is not a theme itself since it is a singular image that recurs and is not in itself one of the "big ideas" related to Revelation of the *Logos* or Response to the *Logos*. Neither does the Spirit fit conveniently with one theme, but in fact plays a role in several themes, including Identity, Life, Witness and Destiny and obliquely in Festival.

The Spirit's place in the Life theme clearly occurs in two places. In his discussion with Nicodemus, the Spirit is connected with the birth from above; "unless someone is born of water and Spirit, he cannot enter the Kingdom of God. That which is born of the flesh is flesh and of the Spirit is spirit" (3:5–6). The Holy Spirit is involved in the new birth. This involvement is not independent from Jesus; to the contrary, Jesus has "the Spirit without measure" (3:34).

The second statement as to the Life-related role of the Spirit comes in 6:63. Following a highly misunderstood Life statement about "eating my flesh" and "drinking my blood" which many listeners take as literal and turn to leave, Jesus corrects their understanding: "the Spirit is the one who makes alive, the flesh profits nothing. The words I speak are spirit and are life." The hearers need to interpret the difficult words of the Bread of Life discourse in a metaphorical way that speaks to the work of the Spirit rather than in any physical sense.

THE CROSS

The cross is Life. John sprinkles this equation throughout the gospel. God gave his only Son (on the cross) so the world might have the possibility of eternal life, so that the world might be saved through him (3:16–17). "The bread which I give is my flesh for the life of the world," Jesus tells the Jews in the Capernaum synagogue (6:51). The flesh and the blood that Jesus gives, he gives on the cross. To the audience in John 10, Jesus says, "I am the good shepherd. The good shepherd lays down his life for the sheep" (10:11, also 15, 17–18; cf. 15:13). In the final moments of his public ministry, Jesus in referring to his impending glorification (on the cross) declares, "Truly, truly I say to you, unless a grain of wheat falls to the earth and dies, it remains alone; but if it dies, it bears much fruit" (12:24). The death of Jesus brings life.

The cross as Life is preeminently illustrated in the testimony of the Beloved Disciple. When the soldier pierced Jesus upon Jesus expiration, the Beloved Disciple witnessed that, "blood and water came out" (19:34). He testified to these two images of Life, "so you might believe."

3

Festival

"**A**RE YOU THE CHRIST?" "Are you Elijah?" "Are you the prophet?" These are questions the Jewish leaders from Jerusalem asked John the Baptist in John 1. Each of these epithets belonged to deliverers from God that the Jewish people were expecting. "The Christ," "Elijah," and "the prophet," all belong to the Festival theme, that theme in the gospel involving all things Jewish, especially the fulfillment of Old Testament expectations.

Perceptive readers of the Gospel of John have long noticed the strong Jewish elements present throughout. The very first words of the gospel, "In the beginning," are a certain allusion to Genesis 1:1. When John tells us that "The Word became flesh and dwelled among us, and we beheld his glory," Jewish readers would immediately discern a reference to the tabernacle and the *shekinah* of the Lord. The gospel mentions Old Testament persons, as well as Jewish festivals, practices, institutions and leaders. Many of the Life theme images used in the gospel such as water, bread, shepherd, wine/vine and others are also Old Testament images; John is almost certainly aware of the OT precedents and assumes as much from his readers.

This Jewish orientation is very intentional on the part of John to the extent that together these elements form a major theme that focuses on Jesus' relationship to Israel and the OT Scriptures. The name of the theme, Festival, relates to some of the key Jewish ritual feasts that Jesus embodies or fulfills, the festivals of Passover, Tabernacles and Sabbath. But "Festival" is only a cipher for Jesus as the fulfillment of all legitimate Jewish expectations as set out in the Old Testament. This theme is preeminently summed up in the identification of Jesus as "the Christ."

Like the other themes, John introduces the Festival theme in the Prologue. And like the Identity and Life themes, the Festival theme points to aspects of Jesus' identity. The former two deal with his divine origin and his saving, life-giving authority, whereas the Festival theme focuses on his identity as the Jewish Messiah. John wants to show the reader that all of the Jewish messianic hopes, as well as the meanings inherent in Jewish laws, rituals, institutions, and feasts are summed up and fulfilled in Jesus. Thus the study of this theme involves attention to OT scripture citations and allusions, OT characters, Jewish rituals, Jewish leaders, Jewish festivals, Torah and its interpretation, as well as traditions current in first century Judaism (and Samaritanism). In addition, a number of titles ascribed to Jesus are specifically related to Jewish messianic ideas.

The Festival theme has both its positive and negative aspects. Positively, Jesus is the fulfillment of everything Jewish ("Salvation is from the Jews"); on the other hand, the Jews reject their Messiah and continue to place their trust in all of their festivals and institutions. This very contrast is present in the Prologue: "he came to his own place, and his own people did not accept him. But whoever did receive him, he gave to them authority to become children of God" (1:11–12). "His own place" and "his own people" refer to the Jewish people in Palestine of the first century AD.

The rejection by "the Jews" in the gospel does not imply a negative aspersion of the Old Testament and everything flowing from it. To the contrary, Jesus' fulfillment of Jewish hopes implies a very positive view of everything Jewish, for God has used his revelation of Torah to prepare for the Jewish Messiah. Once again, the Prologue expresses this very element in verses 16–17: "for from his fullness we have all received grace upon grace, because the law was given through Moses, grace and truth came through Jesus Christ." The phrase "grace upon grace" corresponds with the two phrases of verse 17. The first grace is "the law . . . given through Moses" whereas the second grace is "Grace and truth . . . through Jesus Christ." Jesus thus is seen as the continuation and culmination of the gracious movement of God to reveal himself to humanity.

The importance of the Festival theme is evident from the beginning of the main body of the gospel. As indicated earlier, the narrative of John the Baptist's ministry begins with this theme. When the author invokes the coming of Jewish leaders from Jerusalem, the reader can expect a dialog related to the Festival theme. And indeed that is what transpires with the questions about the Messiah (Christ) or Elijah or the Prophet. All three of these questions are specifically tied to Jewish messianic expectations derived from the Old Testament, and thus the Festival theme.

The scope of the Festival theme in John is nearly overwhelming, because it has so many threads. But a careful understanding of its basic character and its constituent parts leads to a deep understanding of what John was attempting to accomplish in his communication with his own people. Because the Festival theme develops with several different complexes related to Jesus' Jewish identity, I will examine the theme topically. The treatment here will necessarily identify but not delve deeply into aspects of the Festival theme. I encourage you to consult the commentaries listed in the bibliography for further information on any of the elements in this theme.

OLD TESTAMENT IMAGES

"In the beginning . . ." The first words of the gospel jolt the Jewish reader because they allude to the opening words of Genesis 1. Throughout the Gospel of John, the author alludes to Old Testament scripture and images, which breed familiarity among readers aware of those images. An OT allusion is any word, phrase, or concept in the New Testament that recalls a similar word, phrase or concept in the OT.

"The Word" in 1:1 recalls the speech of God in Genesis 1, "And God said . . ." Likewise, John 1:3 recalls the creation narrative and the vast number of reminders of God's creative act throughout the OT. Several scholars have pointed out that John may be alluding to the role of the OT figure of Wisdom in creation and saying that the Word embodies (and is more than) Wisdom. When we reach John 1:4–5, life and light appear, both prominent images beginning with Genesis 1 and repeated throughout the OT. One can also add "darkness" to the list.

When the "Word became flesh" (1:14), John tells us that "he dwelled (Gk. *skenoō*)among us and we beheld his glory (Gk. *doxa*)." These words allude to the tabernacle and to the *shekinah* or glorious presence of God in Exodus and to the promise that God would dwell with his people (such as Ezek 37:27–28). "Full of grace (Gk. *charis*) and truth (Gk. *alētheia*)" alludes to two preeminent characteristics of God in the OT, his loving-kindness (Heb. *hesed*) and truth (Heb. *emet*). If the law was God's guide to his people based on God's character, Jesus Christ embodied God's character in himself.

In this short volume, one cannot begin to name all of the OT allusions in John as part of the Festival theme. As noted earlier, there are many Life theme images that have significant contacts with OT images such as water, bread, wine/vine, shepherd and light. Though these images point to Jesus as the life-giving savior, the images themselves show deep connections with God's abundant provision of life in the OT. The same can be said for images of other themes, such as "I am" in the Identity theme as a reference to Yahweh in the OT. While the primary use of any image may relate to another theme, since the OT is often the source of that image, the image also belongs to the Festival theme.

A survey shows that several images stand out as representative, although this list is not nearly comprehensive. In John 1 the image of the Lamb occurs twice (1:29, 36). The "Lamb of God who takes away the sin of the world," has definite OT sacrificial overtones, and a likely reference to the Passover lamb. A second prominent picture is presented in 1:51 where Jesus virtually quotes from Genesis, "you will see the heavens opened and the angels of God ascending and descending on the Son of Man." Jesus invokes the story of Jacob's ladder (Gen 28:12) with this image and implies that he himself is the ladder to heaven! In John 3:13, Jesus uses the image of the healing serpent on a staff from Exodus as a type of the lifting up of the Son of Man as healing savior of the world. Jacob's well becomes a physical counterpart to the life-giving water that Jesus offers to the Samaritan woman in John 4. So too, the two mountains of Gerazim and Zion function as worship centers to be superseded by "worship in spirit and truth" (4:23). The manna from Moses appealed to by the crowd in chapter 6 as a counterpart to Jesus' feeding miracle, becomes an image that points to Jesus as the "Bread of Life." Jesus' claim to be "Light of the world" in 8:12 evokes many OT passages related to the Lord as light (e. g. Psalm 27:1; Isa 9:1). Likewise, when Jesus claims, "I am the Good Shepherd," he calls to mind a host of OT notions of God as a true shepherd (Gen 48:15; Ps 23; 80:1; Isa 40:11; Ezek 34) and of the nation's leaders as corrupt shepherds (Jer 2:8; 23:1–2; Ezek 34:1–10). Again, when Jesus tells his disciples, "I am the vine," he evinces God as the vine-grower and Israel as the vineyard (Ps 80:8–19; Isa 5:1–7).

The thread running through all of these uses is that Jesus sums up in himself the positive aspects of all of these images.

OLD TESTAMENT FIGURES

The heart of the Festival theme concerns the identity of Jesus as the Jewish Messiah. First century Jewish expectations about a deliverer (or multiple deliverers) that God would send were diverse. John's gospel reflects this diversity in the numerous questions in the gospel about Jesus as Christ (Messiah), Prophet, and king. These deliverer figures were bound up with particular OT persons who acted as types for the deliverers. John names several of the major Old Testament figures in his gospel including Abraham (8:33, 37, 39, 52, 56), Jacob (4:5, 12), Moses (1:17; 1:4; 3:14; 5:45; 6:32; 7:19; 7:22; 8:5; 9:28), David (7:42), and Elijah (1:21, 25), of which the last three were looked to as deliverer figures that would return in some way. References to (the) prophet (1:21, 25; 4:19; 6:14; 7:40, 52; 9:17), (the) Messiah (1:20, 25, 41; 3:28; 4:25, 29; 7:26, 31, 41; 9:22; 11:27; 12:34; 20:31) and (the) king (1:49; 6:15; 12:13, 15; 18:33, 37, 39; 19:3, 12, 19, 21) are dependent on understandings of these past OT figures, especially Moses, David and Elijah.

Another intent of John in including the OT figures is to show that Jesus is greater than these persons along the line of the book of Hebrews. But John is much more subtle about it. He uses comparisons such as in 1:17 (Moses), or questions such as in 4:12 (Jacob) or 8:53 (Abraham) to imply this superiority.

The Patriarchs

The Patriarchs Abraham and Jacob play minor parts in the gospel. Both have questions associated with their presence: "Are you greater than our father Jacob?" in 4:12 and "Are you greater than our father Abraham?" in 8:53. The answer the questioners expect is negative, but John shows that expectation to be false. Jesus is greater than both Abraham and Jacob. Jacob may serve as the builder of the well that has supplied physical water to the people for millennia, but Jesus is "the living water." Abraham may be the father of the Jewish people, but Jesus existed before Abraham and tells the Jews "your father Abraham rejoiced to see my day" (8:56).

Moses, "the Prophet," and Elijah

The most significant OT figure in John is Moses. He is the first OT personage mentioned and the one referred to most often, usually in connection with the Torah, but also in his role as leader of Israel in the wilderness.

References to "the Prophet" in John refer the prophet-like-Moses, one of the messianic figures in the current expectation of the first century.

John portrays Jesus as a sort of antitype to Moses in the first place. As Moses gave the law, Jesus Christ brought grace and truth. This type-antitype does not disparage Moses or the law at all, but does imply that Jesus and the grace and truth that he brings is at the least superior to and at most a full replacement of Moses.

Secondly, Moses as the writer of Torah acts as witness to Jesus in several cases. Philip tells Nathaniel, "we have found the one whom Moses wrote in the law . . ." (1:45). Later in John 5, Jesus is "on trial" for breaking the Sabbath. At the end of the trial Jesus turns the accusation back on his accusers by referring to Moses: "Don't think that I accuse you to the Father. Moses is the one who accuses you, into whom you have put your hope. If you believed Moses, you would believe me, for he wrote about me" (5:45–46).

Jesus draws on Moses as the giver of the law in general (7:19) and in specifics (7:22: "Moses gave you circumcision") to highlight the hypocrisy of the Jewish leaders with regard to their claims to keep the law and place its demands on others.

The Jewish leaders also use Moses as a justification (wrongly in John's opinion) to reject Jesus. In the trial of John 9 the leaders say, "You are a disciple of that man; but we are disciples of Moses; we know that God has spoken to Moses, but we don't know where that one comes from" (9:29). Combined with the material already related in John 5 that Moses wrote about Jesus as well as the constant references to Jesus' origin from God, these words drip with irony as John records them.

Third, there is a connection between Moses and "the Prophet." When the Jewish leaders ask John the Baptist, "Are you the Prophet?" (1:21, cf. 25), they include the definite article that specifies a particular prophet. The crowds conclude that Jesus is "the Prophet" after the feeding of the 5000 (6:14) and at the feast of Tabernacles (7:40). This figure of the Prophet almost certainly comes from Deuteronomy 18:15 where Moses tells the people of Israel, "The Lord God will raise up from among you a prophet like me; you shall heed such a prophet" (NRSV). In John, this "Prophet" is not equated to "the Christ (Messiah)" but seems to be another expected figure alongside the Messiah.[1] This distinction is clear in 7:41 where im-

---

1. The Community Rule of the Dead Sea Scrolls (1QS) mentions three figures in 9:11, "the Prophet" and the "Messiahs of Aaron and Israel."

mediately after some say, "this is truly the Prophet," others say, "this is the Christ." John never makes any specific comment on Jesus as "the Prophet" though the gospel does not preclude that Jesus fulfills this expectation in himself. For John, Jesus is certainly "the Christ" and the fulfillment of all the legitimate hopes associated with that designation.

Elijah only appears in the section on John the Baptist and the Baptist denies the identification. But thereafter the gospel never associates Elijah with Jesus. It is clear from the Synoptic Gospels that some sort of Elijah figure, either as a forerunner or a messianic prophet, would appear. But in John, this speculation goes no further, unless one sees in the miraculous signs some parallel to the deeds of Elijah.

David, Messiah and King

David appears only twice in one verse of John but his appearance there is very significant. During the feast of Tabernacles, after Jesus called out "if anyone thirsts let him come to me and drink" (7:37), John writes (as noted above) that the crowd speculates whether Jesus is either the Prophet or the Christ (7:40–41). Some protested that Jesus could be not the Christ because he was from Galilee, for, "Doesn't scripture say that the Christ comes from the seed of David and from Bethlehem, the town David was from?" (7:42). The inclusion of this question in John shows that the messianic speculation was primarily for a Davidic, royal Messiah. John uses irony with regard to Jesus' place of birth, since his readers likely knew of the tradition of Jesus' birth in Bethlehem (recorded both in Matthew and Luke). From the beginning of the gospel to the end, it is clear that John sees Jesus himself as fulfilling this Jewish expectation of a Davidic Messiah. The purpose statement in 20:31 confirms this assertion: "these things are written so you might believe that Jesus is the Christ."

In reality the entire Festival theme is intended to show that Jesus is the Jewish Messiah. But more specific to the title "Christ" itself, John explores this identification through questions, declarations and implications throughout the gospel. John the Baptist denies the title "Christ," but points to "one whom you don't know who comes after me" (1:26–27). Andrew understands the implications of what the Baptist says and tells Peter, "We have found the Messiah" (1:41). John makes sure the reader sees the equation of "Messiah" to "Christ" in his translation note. Both terms refer to "the anointed one" who would come to deliver Israel. Philip refers to this messianic expectation in 1:45 and then Nathaniel confesses,

"You are the Son of God, you are the King of Israel" (1:49). Nathaniel's statement is a full-blown confession of a royal, Davidic Messiah.

For the reader of John's gospel, what remains is whether the Jewish people as a whole will recognize or reject their Messiah. In John 4, we see a positive recognition of Jesus as the Christ by the Samaritans. Later, Peter makes the confession, "You are the holy one of God" (6:69), which could be a confession of Jesus' divine identity, but is more likely related to his identity as the Jewish Messiah. The clearest confession in John of Jesus' messiahship is from Martha in 11:27: "I believe that you are the Christ, the Son of God who comes into the world." We have here the confession that John desires for all readers of John, that Jesus is "the Christ, the Son of God" (20:31).

On the other hand, ambiguity and negativity provide a counterweight to the positive confessions. In John 7 during the feast of Tabernacles there is rampant speculation as to whether or not Jesus could be the Messiah (7:26–41), and in 10:22–31 the leaders reject the implied affirmative answer to their question, "Tell us plainly if you are the Christ?" (10:24). They even threw anyone out of the synagogue who made this confession (9:22; cf. 12:42; 16:2).

Returning to Nathaniel's confession in 1:49, when "king" is mentioned thereafter in John, the gospel is making a direct connection with the Jewish messianic expectation of a king in the line of David (for example, 12:13, 15). Ultimately the political issues in the trial of Jesus revolved around whether and what kind of "king" Jesus was (18:33–40; 19:12–22). The Jewish leaders argued that Jesus was a rogue political king (19:15), whereas Jesus told Pilate that his "kingdom" was not of this world. When John records that Pilate wrote "King of the Jews" on the placard for the cross, he is demonstrating the extreme irony that Jesus was truly king of the Jews, but one that the people did not want. The identification of Jesus as "King of the Jews" is one John desires his readers to affirm and confess as a constituent element of Jesus "the Christ."

JEWISH INSTITUTIONS

Applying particular OT images to Jesus or showing that Jesus is the fulfillment of the Jewish messianic hopes is only part of how John sets his gospel picture of Jesus within the frame of Judaism. Jesus for John fulfills *all* aspects of the OT. The meanings inherent in Torah, the temple, and the festivals are all summed up in Jesus.

Torah and Scripture

The Torah (Gk. *ho nomos*, usually translated as "the Law") was (and still is) the guiding document for the Jewish people. John shows a deep awareness of this pervasive reality for the Jews of his day. The fact that John introduces the Law in the Prologue expresses the important place John sees for the Law in his understanding of Jesus. The final three verses of the Prologue together set forth the importance of the Law and its limitations. In 1:16–17, John implies that the Law is a gift (a grace, Gk. *charis*) and that Jesus furthers that gift ("grace upon grace"). The Law was given through Moses as a gift of God, grace and truth came through Jesus Christ as the ultimate gift. John in no way denigrates the first gift, but certainly intends Jesus Christ as "grace and truth" to be the perfect fulfillment of everything the Law was intended to accomplish and more. When John goes on to say, "No one has ever seen God; the only begotten God who is in the bosom of the Father has made him known" (1:18), he points to the limitation of the Law (and Moses as representative) in revealing God in his fullness and to Jesus Christ as the very one who can and does reveal God in that fullness.

The gospel sets out Jesus as the actual fulfillment of scripture (Torah and prophets) in very explicit terms. Philip states, "we have found the one whom Moses in the law wrote and in the prophets, Jesus, son of Joseph from Nazareth" (1:45). Jesus states that "[Moses] wrote about me" (5:47), and that Abraham "saw my day" (8:56).

John occasionally quotes scripture with a formula such as "it is written," or "it is written in the prophets," or the like. These quotations invoke the Festival theme almost by definition in most cases. John does not quote the OT nearly as much as the other gospels; he doesn't need to. The pervasive use of the OT in other aspects of the Festival theme show quite clearly that John sees Jesus as the fulfillment of the OT even if there were no direct quotations at all!

When John the Baptist responds to the Jewish leaders in 1:23, he is saying that he and his ministry are a direct fulfillment of Isaiah's prophecy. The disciple's "remembrance" of Psalm 69:9 in 2:17 refers to their grasp of the messianic significance of the scripture. In John 6:31, the crowd invokes scripture only to have Jesus correct their misunderstanding of the text. Jesus himself draws on several short quotations to support his arguments (6:45; 10:34; 15:25), or to show the forthcoming fulfillment of a text (Psalm 41:10 as predicting the betrayal by Judas in John 13:18). The crowds quote scripture at the "triumphal entry" to Jerusalem (12:13).

By far the most prominent use of OT quotations is for the interpretation of Jesus' ministry and death. In several cases, events directly correspond to an OT counterpart (12:15; 19:24, 36, 37). The author draws on Isaiah 6:10 and 53:1 to explain the pervasive negative response to Jesus' ministry (see Destiny theme).

There is a certain negative element in Festival theme with regard to the Torah. The "Jews" in the gospel refuse to consider the possibility that Jesus could fulfill the Torah in himself (5:39). They use their interpretation of Torah as justification for their refusal. "We are disciples of Moses" the leaders say. Sabbath keeping is a key issue for them (5:9–10, 16; 9:13–34). During Jesus' trial they use the "law" as their justification for having Jesus put to death (19:7; cf. 18:31).

Cleansing Rituals

Water is not only an image of the Life theme, but also of the Festival theme as it relates to notions of Jewish cleansing. Ritual cleanness was an extremely important aspect of keeping the Jewish law for observant Jews in the first century. The priesthood involved in the temple sacrifices were scrupulous to keep ritually clean for their tasks, while the Pharisees, a largely lay movement, attempted to stay ritually clean in everyday life as much as possible. The Essenes as evidenced in the Dead Sea Scrolls also diligently sought to maintain ritual purity. Ritual washing using "living water" (water from a spring, a flowing freshwater stream, or even rainwater) was vitally important for this process. The recently discovered Pool of Siloam of the Second Temple period was likely a large pool for ritual cleansing (known as a *mikveh*) in preparation for entering the temple precincts. Converts to Judaism may have gone through a water baptism ritual as a part of the entry process. The Jewish leaders seemed to consider the baptism of John the Baptist as having something to do with messianic expectation.

John the Baptist sets out his baptism ritual as a counterpart to the coming baptism of the Holy Spirit imparted by Jesus (1:33). Beyond that "event," however, the gospel writer portrays Jesus as the fulfillment/replacement of Jewish ritual washing. In the miracle of the water to wine, John notes that Jesus used "six stone jars for the *cleansing of the Jews*" (2:6). When Jesus changes the water to wine, John is arguably setting

Jesus as the one who fulfills and replaces the water cleansing rituals. The wine is likely symbolic of the blood of Jesus on the cross that fulfills and accomplishes all that the Jewish purity system set out to do.

An affirmation of John's concern comes in the next chapter when he writes that a dispute arose with the Jews "about cleansing" (3:25). We learn that people are now going to Jesus and his disciples for baptism (3:26; 4:1). Henceforth, Jesus becomes the source of "living water" which gives life eternally over against the necessity of repeated ritual cleansing required by the Torah (4:14; 7:38). In the upper room before Passover, Jesus washes the disciples feet and tells them, "you are clean" (13:10), then in 15:3 reiterates this reality with "you are already clean through the word I have spoken to you." The word of Jesus has replaced the word of Torah concerning cleansing. The resulting purity is no longer an external one but an internal one.

Temple

John views Jesus as the fulfillment of and replacement for the Jerusalem temple. When John tells us that "the Word became flesh and dwelled among us and we beheld his glory" (1:14), there is an almost certain allusion to the tabernacle and the *shekinah* of God that dwelled there. The first and second temples in Jerusalem were the permanent replacements for the tabernacle and the symbolic place of God's presence. When Jesus clears the temple in John 2 he is declaring the bankruptcy of the physical temple and its apparatus.[2] Then when the Jewish authorities ask him by what authority he cast out the animals and moneychangers, Jesus declared, "Destroy this temple and in three days I will raise it up" (2:19). John then tells us, "He was speaking of the temple of his body." The enactment of the entire scene during Passover along with the reference to "consume me" (2:17) and "destroy" (2:19), point to the cross as the place of ultimate and final sacrifice which renders the temple cultus as no longer necessary.

Later the Samaritan woman speaks of the temple as place of worship (as well as Mt. Gerazim as the Samaritan worship site). Jesus tells her that true worshippers do not worship in particular places but worship the Father in spirit and in truth (4:23). Jesus himself is the locus of the Spirit (1:32; 3:34) and of truth (1:14, 17; 8:31–32). Jesus reinforces

2. Various scholars point to the connections of Jesus' actions with Jer 7:11; Zech 14:21; Mal 3:1–5 et al.

these ideas during the feast of Tabernacles when in the temple itself he relates the water ceremony to the Spirit that he would give (7:37–39) and the light ceremony to himself as "Light of the world" (8:12).

Finally, it is at least notable that a great deal of Jesus' words and interactions in John take place in the temple precincts including 2:14–21; 5:14 and probably the rest of chapter 5; 7:14–44; 8:2–59, and 10:23–29.

Jewish Leaders

The Gospel of John portrays Jesus as the replacement of the Jewish leadership. Throughout this book I have generally translated the term "the Jews" (Gk. *hoi ioudaioi*) as "the Jewish leaders." Though sometimes "the Jews" and "the crowd" are synonymous (6:41, 52; 7:11; 11:31, 36), the context usually indicates the leaders. "Pharisees" and "chief priests" also occur as particular groups of Jewish leaders. In line with the notice in the Prologue that "his own people did not accept him," John indicates that the Jewish leaders almost uniformly reject Jesus.[3] But this rejection highlights John's contention that Jesus himself is the leader of the Jews, *par excellence*, in line with Jesus as Messiah and Prophet. In this particular element of the Festival theme, John develops a dualistic opposition between Jesus as true leader and "the Jews" as false leaders.

Jesus as the true leader comes out in numerous places, most of which are quite pointed. First, in his conversation with Nicodemus, we read that Nicodemus is specifically a "man from the Pharisees, a ruler of the Jews." But in the conversation, Nicodemus is clueless to what Jesus is saying. In an incisive remark, Jesus responds to Nicodemus, "Are you a teacher of Israel and you don't understand these things?" (3:10). He then implies that Nicodemus only understands reality from an earthly, not a heavenly perspective (3:12). Jesus, whom Nicodemus acknowledges as "Rabbi" and "a teacher come from God," is indeed who Nicodemus has begrudgingly confessed.

In John 5:39–47, Jesus accuses the leaders of seeking the glory of one another rather than of God as well as ignoring the scriptures, the very scriptures they claim to follow and guard. Jesus continues this line of thought in 7:19–24, and pointedly tells the leaders in 8:23, "you are from below, I am from above, you are from this world, I am not from this world . . . you will die in your sins."

---

3. Nicodemus, Joseph of Arimathea and a few others would be exceptions, although their loyalty to Jesus is suspect because of fear (see 12:42–43).

The most devastating critique of the Jewish leadership comes in John 10. Following the Pharisees' telling rejection of Jesus' sign of the healing of the blind man in John 9, Jesus speaks directly to them and implies that as leaders they act as "thieves," who come to "steal and kill and destroy" (10:10). They "care" for the sheep only as "hired hands" and leave when danger comes. Jesus on the contrary is "the door of the sheepfold" (10:7) and "the Good Shepherd" (10:11). He is even willing to "lay down his life for the sheep." Jesus as the Good Shepherd alludes to numerous OT passages where God or his representative is shepherd (such as Ps 23:1; 80:2; Num 27:17; Ezek 34:11–16; 37:24). Conversely the leaders of Israel are portrayed as false shepherds in line with Ezek 34:1–10.

In the aftermath of the raising of Lazarus, the Jewish leaders (specifically called "the chief priests and Pharisees") reject that "sign" and begin the plot to kill Jesus (11:47). The leaders ultimately call for Jesus' crucifixion and declare, "we have no king but Caesar" (19:15). Jesus declares however that "my kingdom is not of this world" (18:36), and that he was born "to witness to the truth" (18:37). Alluding to the shepherd of John 10, Jesus continues to Pilate, "everyone who is from the truth hears my voice." From that point on, Pilate calls Jesus "King of the Jews" and places the title onto the cross. At the cross, Jesus becomes the true king, the true leader of the Jews. The leaders themselves are no leaders at all as representatives of God.

JEWISH FESTIVALS

One of the most obvious differences between the first three gospels and John is that Jesus travels to Jerusalem multiple times over his ministry, in every case to attend a Jewish festival (or feast). John makes notice of the festivals of Passover, Tabernacles (or Booths), Dedication (Hanukkah), and an unnamed festival in chapter 5, likely Sabbath. John references Passover ten times with the last six mentioned during Jesus' last week; Tabernacles and Dedication are named once each. Are all of these simply historical references? Apart from the notice of Dedication (10:22), the context in which each occurs would suggest otherwise. While it is historically likely that Jesus would have made his way to Jerusalem for various festivals, it is also evident that John is concerned to show Jesus as the theological fulfillment of these very festivals. John sees Passover as especially important in this regard. This symbolic use of the Jewish festivals is key for the Festival theme and one that adds to the primary focus of the theme on the identity of Jesus as the fulfillment of all Jewish messianic hopes.

With regard to Passover and Tabernacles, John makes deep symbolic connections between the import of each feast and the person of Jesus. The feasts of Passover/Unleavened Bread and Tabernacles were the two principle festivals of the Jews corresponding to the first grain harvest and the harvest of grapes and olives respectively, where they celebrated the provision of God through specific offerings and sacrifices laid out in Exodus, Leviticus, and Deuteronomy. But much of the theological importance developed in their connection to the Exodus and the forty years in the wilderness. With regard to Sabbath, John shows Jesus to be "lord of the Sabbath" (though these are words of the Synoptic Gospels).

Sabbath

Sabbath was a weekly feast for the Jews. It was one of the defining characteristics of Jewish practice in the ancient world. For the Jews, the weekly day of rest connected them to the very creation of the world as set out in Genesis. And, of course, the Sabbath rest was a key statute of the Ten Commandments. For the rabbis of the post-exilic period into the first century AD, the proper keeping of Sabbath was of highest importance in expressing obedience and devotion to God. As such, the rabbis minutely defined what constituted "work" on the Sabbath and sought to impose their definitions in the Jewish regions of Palestine. This background sets the stage for the Sabbath as a part of the Festival theme in John.

In John 5, Jesus heals a lame man on the Sabbath. As pointed out earlier, the miraculous sign focused on the Life theme: Jesus made the man "well." The Jewish leaders first of all objected to the man's carrying his mat on the Sabbath, but later turned their ire toward Jesus. In response to their questioning Jesus states, "My Father is working until now and I am working" (5:17). John tells us that "the Jewish leaders sought all the more to kill him, not just because he broke the Sabbath, but he also called God his own Father, thus making himself equal to God" (5:18). Jesus' subsequent remarks, though intending on the surface to dispel this charge, actually show Jesus to have the same Sabbath prerogatives as God according to the rabbis. God, according to their discussions, rested in every way on the Sabbath except for giving life and judging. As I pointed out in the Identity theme, the reasoning was that births and deaths continued on the Sabbath, thus God gave life and judged.

Jesus tells the Jewish leaders, "Just as the Father has life in himself, so too he gave the Son to have life in himself. And he gave authority to him to make judgment, because he is the Son of Man" (5:26–27). Jesus has authority to heal on the Sabbath if he so desires.

The discussion about Sabbath during Tabernacles in John 7:19–24 is actually a continuation of the discussion about the healing of the lame man (7:21). Jesus uses a rabbinical form of argument, "from the lesser to the greater," to argue that since Jews circumcised on the Sabbath to keep the law, shouldn't the act of healing be acceptable also? Jesus sets himself as the right interpreter of what it means to keep Sabbath.

Sabbath as a point of contention continues with the healing of the blind man in John 9. There the Pharisees interrogate the man again and again, refusing to accept the legitimacy of the miracle because it happened on the Sabbath. Jesus is simply a sinner to them. The healed blind man rejoins with "we know that God does not hear sinners, but if anyone is godly and does his will he hears them. No one has ever heard that someone has healed a person blind from birth. If this man were not from God, he would be able to do nothing" (9:31–33). The Pharisees threw the man out, but the point is clearly made that Jesus has the right and ability to heal on the Sabbath.

John mentions the Sabbath four more times (19:31 twice; 20:1, 19). Jesus was crucified on a Friday, in this instance the Preparation Day for the Passover. This particular year, Passover fell on a Sabbath, thus making it a "great Sabbath" (19:31). Jesus death and burial took place prior to the fall of evening, thus even though Jesus gave life on the Sabbath during his life, he rested on Sabbath in his death. Jesus' resurrection took place on the first day of the week, after the Sabbath.

Tabernacles

The festival of Tabernacles (Gk. *skēnopēgia*) took place soon after the Day of Atonement in the month of Tishri (October–November). The festival had developed a very dense repertoire of meaningful symbolism over the centuries, one of which remembered the provision of God for the Israelites in the wilderness. A daily water ceremony corresponded with prayers for early rain. At night four giant menorahs lit up the night sky, perhaps recalling the fiery cloud in the wilderness. The prophet Zechariah saw Tabernacles as a proleptic celebration of the messianic age where "it will be one continuous day" and when "living waters will issue from Jerusalem" (Zech 14:7–8 NRSV). Jesus proclaims himself as the fulfillment of these promises.

John 7–8 takes place during Tabernacles and the narrative is full of Festival theme material (as well as all the other themes). The feast is not only named but referred to five more times during the course of chapter 7, including notices of the middle and last days of the feast. In addition there is major material on the interpretation of Moses and the Torah with relation to circumcision and healing on the Sabbath (7:19–24), as well as Abraham as witness to Jesus (8:30–58). In the first of these passages, Jesus presents himself as the definitive interpreter of the Torah instead of the Jewish leaders. One further prominent Festival theme motif is the questioning of whether Jesus is the Prophet or the Messiah (7:40–41).

The narrative has two other key elements directly related to the feast of Tabernacles. First, John writes that, "on the last day, the great day of the feast, Jesus stood and cried out saying, If anyone thirsts, let him come to me. The one who believes in me, just as it is written, out of his belly shall flow rivers of living water" (7:37–38). John goes on to say that the word regarded the giving of the Spirit. This passage is notorious for its interpretive difficulties, but with regard to the Festival theme, there appears a clear connection between Jesus' words about himself as the source of "living waters" and the daily water ceremony of the feast of Tabernacles, where on the last day the priests walked around the altar seven times as part of the ceremony. Second, while in the temple (8:20), Jesus proclaims himself as "the Light of the World" (8:12) during the feast where huge menorahs in the Court of Women lit Jerusalem at night.

Passover

The Passover feast brought to remembrance the deliverance of the first-born in Egypt when each Israelite family sacrificed a lamb and put some of its blood on their doorpost. In *every case* where John mentions Passover, the surrounding context makes some sort of reference to the death of Jesus. John, in fact, gives us at least one preliminary clue that the theological significance of Passover is important. When John the Baptist recognizes Jesus in 1:29, he declares, "Behold, the Lamb of God who takes away the sin of the world." Though some scholars argue for an "apocalyptic Lamb" or a reference to the Suffering Servant, the Paschal Lamb is arguably the primary image here. It is not yet clear that this identification refers to Jesus' death, but the association of Lamb and sin here suggests some type of sacrificial death. Thereafter when Passover is mentioned, there is either direct or indirect allusion to the coming death of Jesus.

In 2:13, Jesus is in Jerusalem for his first Passover visit in the gospel. At that time he carried out the "cleansing of the Temple." In the aftermath, Jewish leaders ask Jesus what authority he had to do this deed and he responds in 2:20, "Destroy this temple and in three days I will raise it." As noted earlier, we have a notice of Jesus' replacing the Jewish temple here. But we also have a notice of Jesus' death, as John tells us in the following verse, "He was speaking of the temple of his body." Then almost directly, John mentions Passover once again in 2:23: "And while he was in Jerusalem at the Passover festival, many believed in his name."

Notice of the succeeding year's Passover comes in 6:4 when Jesus is in Galilee just prior to the miracle of the fish and loaves. One might argue that the immediate context has nothing to do with Jesus' death. However, as one reads chapter six there is a conversation between Jesus and the Jews concerning God's provision of bread (manna) in the exodus and Jesus as the "bread from heaven." Later, Jesus makes the audacious statement that "the bread which I will give is my flesh for the life of the world" (6:51), which is followed up with, "unless you eat the flesh of the Son of Man and drink his blood, you do not have life in yourselves" (6:53). Though the exegesis of this passage is difficult, most scholars see a reference to the death of Jesus and ultimately to the Christian Eucharist. The timeframe of the Passover lends a further theological layer to the discussion; the "Lamb of God who takes away the sin of the world" now gives his flesh "for the life of the world." Jesus carries out this act the following year at the Passover festival in Jerusalem.

The next announcement of Passover is, in fact, that of the Passion Week. Directly after the raising of Lazarus in chapter 11 with the subsequent counsel of Caiaphus that Jesus must be put to death, John tells us that, "the Passover of the Jews was near" (11:55). The people wondered whether Jesus would come (11:56) and the leaders plotted how to arrest him (11:57). Meanwhile, "six days before Passover Jesus came to Bethany where Lazarus was whom Jesus raised from the dead" (12:1). Mary then anoints Jesus' feet with perfume for "the day of my burial" (12:6). Immediately afterward, John tells us that the Jewish leaders plotted to kill both Jesus and Lazarus. The subsequent narrative of chapter 12 shows Jesus' realization that the "hour" of his death was imminent.

Finally, in the initiation of the second half of John (chapters 13–21) John states, "Before the feast of Passover, Jesus, knowing that his hour had come to pass from this world to the Father, and having loved his own who were in the world, he loved them to the end." "His own" were the disciples and Jesus spends the next five chapters preparing them for his death and departure. Some have spoken of the gospel of Mark as being a passion account with an extended introduction. This observation may be even more apropos to John! John makes sure that the entirety of this section is understood as happening during the Passover.

The account of Jesus' arrest and crucifixion in John takes place on the Preparation Day for Passover. The three notices to Passover itself in John 18–19 are studies in contrast for the Festival theme. In the first, the Jewish leaders do not enter Pilate's quarters so they "wouldn't be defiled and could eat the Passover meal" (18:28). John's sense of irony is in full display here. When Pilate asks whether he should release the "King of the Jews" to fulfill the custom at Passover, everyone called for the release of Barabbas instead. Subsequently at the eighth hour of the Preparation Day for the Passover (19:14) Pilate declares, "Behold your king," and the leaders cried out for Jesus to be crucified. This series of events took place at the very hour the priests in the Temple were slaughtering the Passover lambs. Perhaps it is needless to say, but the cross as an element of the Festival theme is in perfect focus at this point.

CONCLUSION

The Festival theme runs deeply in the flow of John from beginning to end. Much of the theme is clear on the surface, but much more is part of the undercurrents in John. It cannot always be seen, but its influence is there. Matthew is often viewed as the most Jewish of the gospels, but John surely equals or surpasses Matthew's Jewish bent. John has a deep desire to show his own people that Jesus is truly the Messiah for whom they have yearned for so long.

4

Witness

"**W**HAT IS TRUTH?" IS the question that Pilate rhetorically poses to Jesus during his trial. Pilate's question may be a cynical one, but the question itself is one that John wants us to ask as we read the gospel. From the first verses of the Prologue to the very end of the gospel, truth is a guiding concern for John. Truth for John is not a static philosophical idea or body of rational propositions; truth for John resides in, and actually is, the person of Jesus as the revealer of God. John declares in the Prologue "we beheld his glory . . . full of grace and truth" (1:14), and Jesus tells his disciples, "I am the way, the truth and the life" (14:6).

The motif of truth is one of a complex of images and motifs belonging to the Witness theme. Broadly speaking, the Witness theme is concerned with Truth and various forms of testimony to the Truth. The vocabulary for this theme is fairly clear. Verbs include, "send," "confess," and "witness (or testify)," while nouns include "truth" and "witness." Adjectives and adverbs ("true," "truly") also add to the theme. Verbs of speech such as "say," or "cry out," or "answer" often introduce statements of Witness.

But the Witness theme is not as simple as identifying vocabulary. The content of a person's witness must also be considered, such as the witness of the Samaritan woman when she goes into town and proclaims, "Come see a man to told me everything I've done. Could this be the Christ?" (4:29). She and her words become examples of the Witness theme, though the vocabulary of witness is absent. Later in that particular scenario, the theme does become explicit when John relates that, "many from that city believed in him because of the word of the woman *witnessing* that, 'he told me everything I had done'" (4:39). This explicit language does not always occur, however.

Another remarkable aspect of the Witness theme is its dual nature with regard to Revelation and Response. On the Revelation side, Jesus is the witness to the Father and to himself as sent from the Father. This truth (pun intended) is highly evident in the Prologue and recurs over and over again throughout the gospel, especially in the language of the Father "sending" the Son. This sending terminology is a form of diplomatic speech where an appointed emissary takes an approved message or action to a recipient. The emissary acts on behalf of the sender and is a "true witness" if the emissary faithfully carries out the appointed task. In the gospel, Jesus receives words and tasks from the Father and proclaims and carries them out faithfully. Another way of expressing this task is "mission."

On the Response side, people witness to Jesus. The first is John the Baptist. As the gospel proceeds, various people who encounter Jesus go on to testify about him to others, sometimes in surprising ways. And not only people, but also God, the Spirit, the scriptures and Jesus' "signs" testify about Jesus.

Finally there is a passing on of witness from Jesus to his followers in the so-called Farewell Discourses and especially in the John 17 prayer. The most unmistakable instance of this "passing the torch" motif is in the Upper Room following the resurrection when Jesus says, "As the Father has sent me, I also send you" (20:21). For those developing a biblical theology of mission, the Gospel of John may have the clearest expression of such a theology.

PROLOGUE

The Prologue vividly introduces both the Revelation and Response aspects of the Witness theme. The *Logos* become flesh is witness to God the Father and John the Baptist is witness to the *Logos*.

The Witness theme arguably begins in John 1:1, though these initial words of John better fit with the Identity theme. By its very nature, the Word (*Logos*) is witness. The Word is the very communication from God and about God. Throughout the gospel, John wants the reader to know that the words that Jesus speaks are the words of God. A number of phrases in the Prologue set the stage for this reality, though not necessarily with Witness language. First, "the light shines in the darkness" (1:5). This light is the "true light, who enlightens all people" (1:9). The Life theme is obviously evident here, but the language of truth and the action of light shining is consistent with Witness. Indeed, the incarnate Word is full of grace and *truth* (1:14, 17).

The Prologue also exhibits the effectiveness of the Word's witness both implicitly and explicitly. When John writes in 1:14, "And the Word became flesh and dwelled among us and we beheld his glory . . . full of grace and truth," he expresses the effective witness of the Word to the Father. John makes this authoritative witness explicit in 1:18: "No one has ever seen God; the only-begotten God who is in the bosom of the Father has made him known." The term John uses for "made known" (Gk. *exēgeomai*) occurs only here in the Gospel, but sums up well the task of Jesus' witness to God. From this point on, Jesus is the Witness who speaks for God (and who testifies about himself as God!).

John introduces the Response aspect of the Witness theme with the distinct language of the theme in the intriguing insertion about John the Baptist in 1:6–8. Many scholars believe that these words originally appeared prior to 1:19. In putting these verses here, however, the gospel writer shows John the Baptist as a witness to the *Logos* prior to his appearance in the person of Jesus Christ. The key terms "sent" (Gk. *apostellō*), "testify" (Gk. *martyreō*) and "witness" (noun, Gk. *martyria*) appear: "There was a man *sent* from God whose name was John. He came as a *witness* to *testify* about the Light . . . He was not the light, but [came] to *testify* about the light." These three terms, along with the other Greek term for "send," *pempō*, prove to be the most common words for the theme throughout the gospel.[1] Later in 1:15, John brings the confession of the Baptist from 1:30 into the Prologue and introduces the confession with Witness language. After the notice of the incarnation in 1:14, we read, "John *testifies* about him and cried out saying, 'the one coming after me is of greater rank than me, because he existed before me.'" In this instance one should notice not just the *language* of witness, but also the *content* of the testimony. When others testify about Jesus, the substance of the testimony normally consists of statements about who Jesus is and typically conforms to one of the first three themes, Identity, Life, or Festival. In this case, the content of the Baptist's testimony is part of the Identity theme.

---

1. A concordance analysis shows that John uses these terms far more frequently than other NT writers. The Johannine letters are consistent with the gospel in this regard.

"I AM . . . THE TRUTH"

In a broad sense, Jesus as *the* Witness is indicated every time Jesus speaks a word or performs an action. Jesus testifies about the Father, about the relationship between himself and the Father, about himself and about others. The scope of Jesus as Witness is impossible to illustrate comprehensively since examples occur in some way in every chapter of John; a few representative instances must suffice.

Fundamental to the Witness theme is Jesus' claim to speak the truth. His distinctive use of the clause, "Truly, truly, I say to you" (Gk. *amēn amēn legō hymin*), implies this claim. In John, Jesus uses this phrase twenty five times to introduce solemn statements of truth. The clause essentially says, "Listen up, what I am about to say is very important (and true)." The content of these statements invariably belongs to one or another (or combination) of the seven themes. In John 3, for example, this phrase introduces a statement from the Witness and Believing themes when Jesus tells Nicodemus, "Truly, truly I say to you that what we know we speak, and what we have seen we testify, but you do not receive our witness" (3:11).

Throughout the gospel Jesus explicitly claims to speak the truth (7:18; 8:40, 45; 18:37) and makes the remarkable statement to his disciples, "I am the way, the truth, and the life" (14:6). At one point the Pharisees accuse Jesus with, "You are testifying about yourself; your testimony is not true" (8:13). Jesus responds, "If I testify about myself, my testimony is true because I know where I come from and where I am going" (8:14). Jesus invokes his Identity as the basis for his true witness. In the many discourses throughout the gospel, Jesus makes stunning claims for himself, particularly evident in "I am" statements whether absolute (see Identity) or with a predicate (see Life). Jesus makes these claims based on his relationship to the Father as the one who sent him.

Jesus as Witness often speaks a word of truth about humans, whether particular individuals, groups, or "the world." In chapter one, Jesus declares a new name for Simon—Cephas—which John goes on to translate as "Peter" (Gk. *petros* meaning rock). A few verses later Jesus says of Nathaniel, "Look! a true Israelite in whom there is no guile" (1:47). These statements of truth about particular individuals occur throughout John: Nicodemus (3:10), the Samaritan woman (4:17), the royal official (4:48—though this instance might be seen as a provocation to faith rather than a witness statement), Judas (6:70; 13:21), and Peter

(13:38; 21:18). John makes a particular comment about Jesus' perception of people in 2:24–25: "But Jesus himself did not entrust himself to them because he knew everything, indeed he had no need for anyone to *testify* about a person, for he knew what was in a person."

This straightforward telling the truth about people extends to the "crowds" (6:26), and to the Jewish leaders, the usual referent of the phrase "the Jews." Perhaps the most extreme example is Jesus telling them in 8:44, "You are from your father the devil." Regarding his reception by the Jewish people, "Jesus *testified* that a prophet has no honor in his own country" (4:43).

In its widest frame, Jesus testifies the truth about the world. When Jesus speaks to his brothers in response to their request for him to show himself in Jerusalem at Tabernacles, he incisively states: "The world is not able to hate you, but it hates me, because I *testify* about [the world] that its deeds are evil" (7:7).

JESUS AS "THE SENT ONE"

John carries out a seemingly peculiar strategy in his gospel. Jesus is the supreme witness to God the Father, but in his witness to the Father, he is also witnessing about himself. John 1:18 embeds this peculiarity in its distinctive combination of words: "The only-begotten God who is in the bosom of the Father has made him known." God the Son reveals God the Father. In doing so, the Son reveals himself to be God.

Beginning with the important passage in 3:16–18, the motif of God the Father sending the Son becomes prominent throughout the rest of the gospel, especially in chapters 1–12. In John 3:16, we read that, "God loved the world in this way, that he gave his only Son." "Gave" (Gk. *didōmi*) here embeds both the incarnation and the cross. In the next verse, John changes the language slightly: "For God did not *send* (Gk. *apostellō*) his Son into the world to judge the world but that the world might be saved through him" (3:17). Here John introduces "sending" language to the same effect. The salvation of the world comes with the presence of the Son in the incarnation and the mission of the Son that is completed on the cross. This "sending of the Son" must always be read with John's overall thesis in mind: God loves the world and has sent his Son to save the world.

That the Son actually represents God (1:18) becomes clearer in 3:31–36, a passage dense with Witness language. Jesus is the one who "comes from above" (31), who "witnesses what he has seen and heard" (32), for "the one whom God has sent speaks the words of God, for He gives the Spirit without measure" (34). This sending is not just an impersonal one, but is based in the reality that "the Father loves the Son and has given all things into his hand" (35). The Son is the *personal* emissary of the Father.

When Jesus speaks from this point forward in the gospel, especially to "the Jews" (whether the Jewish leaders or the crowds), he often refers to God as "the Father who sent me" or "He who sent me."[2] He also refers to God this way to his own disciples, particularly in "farewell speeches" in 13–17.[3] In relaying this particular manner that Jesus refers to God, John is representing Jesus, not only as sent from God, but the true representative of God to humanity. At points throughout the gospel, John includes statements reiterating that the words of Jesus are the very words of God (5:24; 7:16; 8:26; 12:49). With these statements in mind, we as readers may be mildly amused when Philip asks in 14:8, "Show us the Father." Jesus responds, "The one who has seen me has seen the Father" (14:9). He goes on, "Don't you believe that I am in the Father and the Father is in me? The words which I speak to you, I don't speak from myself, but the Father who abides in me does his work" (14:10).

WITNESSES TO JESUS

There are many witnesses to Jesus in the gospel, and not only people. God, Scripture and the signs are all witnesses to Jesus in addition to many different people.

The first and quintessential human witness to Jesus is John the Baptist. As I pointed out earlier, he is the very first witness in the gospel (1:6–8). The remainder of John 1 (1:19–51) shows a series of witnesses to Jesus beginning with John the Baptist, who testifies about the coming of one "of whom I am not worthy to loose the thong of his sandals." The Baptist proclaims Jesus as "the Lamb of God," "the one who ranks ahead of me," "the one who baptizes with the Holy Spirit," and "the Son of God." John the Baptist also points out Jesus to two of his disciples, who then start a chain of witness, beginning with Andrew's witness to Peter and then Philip's witness to Nathaniel. The content of the testimony in

2. John 5:23, 24, 30, 33, 36, 37, 38; 6:29, 38, 39, 44, 57; 7:16, 18, 28, 29; 8:16, 18, 26, 29, 42; 10:36; 11:42; 12:44, 45, 49.

3. John 4:34; 9:4; 13:20; 14:24, 26; 15:21; 16:5; 17:3, 8, 18, 21, 25; 20:21.

every case has to do with the identity of Jesus, primarily in relation to the Festival theme. Jesus is the "Messiah," "the one about whom Moses and the prophets wrote," and finally with the testimony of Nathaniel, "the Son of God," and "the king of Israel." Jesus is a witness to others in this chapter (Peter in 1:42; Nathaniel, 1:47) and even to himself (1:51).

These instances in John 1 set the tone for other witnesses to come in the gospel including John the Baptist again in 3:27–30, the Samaritan woman in 4:28–29 (and the Samaritans in 4:42), the healed lame man in 5:15, Peter in 6:28–29 and the healed blind man throughout John 9. Martha makes the model confession in 11:27. Nicodemus makes a valiant attempt at witness in 7:50 and ultimately makes an implicit statement of witness by participating in Jesus' burial with Joseph of Arimathea (19:39–41). Mary Magdalene "went and proclaimed to the disciples that 'I have seen the Lord' and the things he told her" (20:18).

Several times throughout the gospel, the Witness theme takes on a judicial bent, wherein actual witnesses are called upon to testify. John 5 is an especially rich example. Jesus is on trial for breaking the Sabbath and "for calling God his own Father, thus making himself equal with God" (5:18). After defending himself by insisting that he is only doing what the Father has told him and given him authority to carry out, Jesus calls four witnesses before the Jewish leaders. First, he calls the human witness, John the Baptist (5:31–35), in light of the respect the people gave John. Next he calls upon his "works" as a witness (5:36). These primarily consist of the miraculous signs (see the Signs theme), and give proof that the Father did indeed send Jesus. Subsequently, Jesus actually calls on God the Father as a witness (5:37) but tells his hearers that they are unable to hear or see that witness because they don't believe in Jesus (5:39)! Finally, Jesus invokes the OT scriptures as a witness (5:39), but the hearers desire not to come to Jesus impedes their understanding of that witness too. In a final twist to this trial, Jesus changes from defendant to prosecutor. He calls on Moses as the witness who "will accuse you," for "if you had believed Moses you would believe me, for that one wrote about me" (5:46). Moses' writings themselves are a testimony.

Another remarkable example of a Witness trial occurs in John 9. Jesus is on trial as "a sinner" *in absentia* for breaking the Sabbath (9:16, 24). The actual defendant is the blind man Jesus had healed. The chapter shows a series of successive scenes where the man is called upon to testify what had happened to him, first to his neighbors, then in the formal setting of a hearing before a panel of Pharisees. Throughout the chapter the man tells what Jesus did for him (9:11, 15, 25). As the man testifies again and again, his understanding of Jesus grows, first as "a prophet" (9:17), then as one whom God listens to (9:31), and finally as "the Son of Man" (9:36–38). The irony is that as the man testifies and his faith and understanding grows, the Pharisees refuse to accept that testimony even though the evidence of what Jesus had done was irrefutable.

One mysterious witness is present in John, the "disciple whom Jesus loved." This individual is important because he is the witness behind the entire Gospel of John and the likely writer of at least the first twenty chapters. The penultimate verse of the gospel is clear about the Witness role of this disciple: "This is the disciple who testifies about these things and who has written these things, and we know his testimony is true" (21:24). This disciple does not appear by the moniker "beloved disciple" until the last supper, but may be the unnamed disciple of John the Baptist and companion of Andrew in 1:37–39. He appears with the other disciples at the last supper and reclined next to Jesus (13:23–25). This disciple was likely the one with Peter when Jesus was arrested and taken to the high priest's residence (18:15). The gospel tells us that he was known to the high priest. Once again this "disciple whom Jesus loved" appears at the cross and takes on the care of Jesus' mother at Jesus' request (19:26–27). Moments later, this disciple witnessed and testified to the death of Jesus with these words: "But one of the soldiers stabbed his side with a spear and out came blood and water, and the one who has seen has testified and his testimony is true, and he knows that he speaks truth, so you might also believe" (19:34–35). He along with Peter witnesses the empty tomb, is presumably with the other disciples when Jesus appears in John 20, and then sees the resurrected Jesus again by the Sea of Galilee in John 21. This disciple has traditionally been identified as John, the son of Zebedee, though a number of scholars have posited Lazarus, or an unknown disciple. Nonetheless, this disciple bases the authenticity of the gospel account he has written on his testimony as an eyewitness to the life, death, and resurrection of Jesus.

MISSION

There is a progression in the movement of the Witness theme: Jesus is a witness to God; Jesus' followers are witnesses of Jesus (as God) to the world. To this point, we have seen how this basic movement works within the Gospel of John, though the progression is obviously more complex than two simple steps. Thus far, this movement is only evident within the life and ministry of Jesus. The whole notion of Jesus as "the Sent One" implies that he had a mission from God. We also see that those who had responded to Jesus make confessions about him to others. But John extends the Witness theme with a view beyond the gospel proper; those who believe in Jesus are to testify to this reality after Jesus has departed.

The initial foray into this aspect of the Witness theme occurs in John 4, though by pattern, John 1:19–51 is also useful. In a sort of intermission in the story of Jesus and the Samaritan woman (who is herself an ideal example of the mission impulse), Jesus' disciples return from town with food. When offered the food, Jesus refuses, because "I have food that you do not know about . . . my food is to do the will of the one who sent me and to complete his work" (4:32, 34). Jesus himself has a mission and receives deep joy in its fulfillment. He goes on to speak of a harvest (4:35) and the disciples' part in that harvest (4:36–37). Then Jesus concludes, "I sent you to reap what you did not work for; others have worked and you have entered into their labor" (4:38). Here Jesus is proleptically commissioning the disciples for their future work.

The mission idea proper develops in the last half of John in Jesus' instruction to his disciples in chapters 13–16, in Jesus' prayer in John 17, and during the resurrection appearances of John 20–21. John 20:21 has the most succinct statement of mission: "Just as the Father has sent me, I also am sending you." In chapters 13–17 Jesus lays out the basic principles of this mission, including internal and external aspects, as well as the means for accomplishing the mission.

After Jesus washes the feet of the disciples at the last supper, he tells them, "If I, your Lord and Teacher, have washed your feet, you also should wash the feet of one another . . . Truly, truly I say to you, a slave is not greater than his master, nor a sent one greater than the one who has sent him" (13:14, 16). Jesus thus presents the thesis that his disciples should follow in his steps.

The internal aspect of the mission is that the followers of Jesus should love one another, in line with Jesus' washing of their feet: "Just as I have loved you, so also you should love one another" (13:34). Why? Because love for one another is essential for the external mission to the world: "By this everyone will know that you are my disciples, if you have love for one another" (13:35).

In his prayer to the Father in John 17, Jesus acknowledges that he has completed his work of making the Father known to the disciples. Now he prays that the Father "would keep them in your name which you have given me, so that they might be one" (17:11). Why? Though the world hates them as they hated Jesus (17:14), Jesus prays, "Just as you have sent me into the world, I also have sent them into the world" (17:18). The mission of the disciples is to be "one" together with the Father and the Son "so that the world might believe that you sent me" (17:20–21).

The means for accomplishing the mission comes from "abiding" in Jesus and his words (15:1–17), and also through the work of the Paraclete or Holy Spirit. The Spirit is a multi-themed motif in John that plays a part in the Identity, Life, Festival and Destiny themes. The Spirit also plays a vital role in the Witness theme. The Spirit is the "Spirit of truth" (14:7) who will "teach you all things and remind you of everything I told you" (14:26). The Spirit acts as a witness to Jesus (15:26). Moreover, the Spirit "will convict the world about sin and about righteousness and about judgment" (16:8) and "will lead you in all truth" (16:13). Everything that Jesus desires for his followers to carry out is based on what the Spirit will accomplish in and through them. When Jesus stated his commission to the disciples in 20:21, he "breathed on them and said to them 'Receive that Holy Spirit'" (20:22). Jesus' charge to the disciples is bound together with the Spirit's empowerment for the charge.

CONCLUSION

The Witness theme is at once complex, yet focused. John desires to highlight truth and witness in his gospel as inherent in the person of Jesus as the true Witness to the Father, to himself as the Father's emissary, and indeed to himself as one with the Father. Jesus' ultimate testimony took place on the cross, where in finishing the work God gave him, he testified to the entire world that God loves them. John also wants to show that transformed believers in Jesus naturally become witnesses to that very truth. They testify to this transformation by loving one another and by proclaiming the Truth to all people.

5

Believing

"**D**O YOU BELIEVE IN the Son of Man?" This question of Jesus to the healed blind man in John 9:35 is the question that John asks of all the readers of his gospel. But the question is not such a simple one. John actually asks, do you *really* believe? Some say they believe, but their continued faithfulness to Jesus becomes questionable.

The Believing theme is the primary counterpart to the identity of Jesus as set out in the Identity, Life, Festival, and Witness themes. This theme adheres most closely to the Response meta-theme. John introduces Believing in the Prologue and develops it consistently throughout the gospel. We detect the theme in three of the most well known verses of the gospel, 1:12, 3:16 and 20:31. In each of these instances John highlights the response of believing as the means to eternal life and becoming a child of God. In the last of these examples, John clearly states the theme: "But these are written so that you may come to believe that Jesus is the Christ, the Son of God, and that through believing you might have life in his name." John's desire in writing his gospel is that readers would respond to what he writes about Jesus by placing their faith in him. What placing faith in Jesus entails, however, is much more than simply an intellectual endorsement. To believe for John means not only to believe that Jesus is the Messiah and Son of God as a concept, but even more, to express that mental acceptance by whole-hearted devotion of one's life to Jesus.

"Believing" (Gk. *pisteuō*) may be the primary term for John with regard to this acceptance, but believing is only one a whole host of terms that add to the theme.[1] The most prominent are the verbs "seeing" (Gk. *blepō, oraō,* and *theaomai*) and "knowing" (Gk. *ginōskō* and *oida*) Others

---

1. Throughout this chapter I will give the (transliterated) Greek term only the first time I refer to a verb in this theme.

are comprehend, accept or receive, behold, hear, follow, seek, honor, ask, come, remain (stay, abide), find, remember, enter, eat, and drink, though even this list may not be exhaustive! The complex of words that John uses is intentional; he wants to show that becoming a follower of Jesus indicates an initiation of faith and devotion that matures into a life fully consecrated to the person of Jesus and God the Father. This fully consecrated life is the expression of the gift of "eternal life" in the present. One caveat is in order; though John uses a wide range of vocabulary to develop the Believing theme, the mere presence of one of these terms does not automatically add to the theme because John also uses some of the words in their simple, physical sense. This observation is particularly pertinent with verbs of sensing such as seeing or hearing, or the common verb, come. Nonetheless, John may at times imply a deeper level than the physical when using these words in their ordinary sense. For example, in John 1:29, John the Baptist "sees" Jesus coming physically, but also "sees" who he is as "the Lamb of God."

The Believing theme takes two primary trajectories in the gospel, one positive and one negative. The positive intent of the revelation of the Father in Jesus is the restoration or rebirth of humanity. Those that respond to the revelation fulfill this intent. The response involves both initiation *and* maintenance. While the commencement of a commitment is absolutely essential in John's understanding, if that commitment is not followed by continued dedication it is no legitimate response at all. The use of terms such as follow (Gk. *akoloutheō*), remain (Gk. *menō* also rendered "continue," "abide" or "stay"), and remember (Gk. *mimnēskō*), suggest the perseverance of this commitment beyond its initiation. A remarkable feature of most of the verbs is their tense; throughout John, the verbs that are significant for this theme are usually in the present or imperfect tenses in Greek. These tenses encode what grammarians call "continuous" or "durative" action. Though for stylistic purposes, most translations render these with simple action (i.e. "believe") instead of durative action (i.e. "are believing"), it is important to understand that the preponderance of these tenses indicates a persistent, habitual dedication to Christ.[2] The aspects of initiation and maintenance are both

2. A particularly illustrative example of the distinction between initiation and maintenance occurs in 8:30–32: "As he was saying these things, many believed in him. Then Jesus said to the Jews who had believed in him, 'If you continue in my word, you are truly my disciples; and you will know the truth, and the truth will make you free.'"

emphasized in the so-called "Book of Signs" (1:19–12:50), whereas the maintenance aspect is emphasized in the so-called "Farewell Discourse" (13–17) and chapters 20–21. The Believing theme is restricted in the passion narrative in John 18–19, though still present at some key points.

In contrast to the positive responses, there is a thread of negative response throughout the gospel; many do not believe the claims of Jesus. They do *not* see, or believe or comprehend or receive, or follow, etc. We have already seen this dualism in the negative side of the Life theme (such as darkness) and will see a negative side to the Signs theme and especially the Destiny theme (in the reality of judgment). Even in John 3:16 we see the implied results of not believing: "that whoever believes in him should not perish." Throughout the gospel, John gives abundant examples of those who respond in a negative way. In fact, the negative trajectory is arguably more prominent than the positive trajectory. I will comment on the implications of this prominence after giving appropriate examples.

Although the emphasis of the Believing theme is on the response of people to Jesus, John also portrays Jesus as responding positively to the Father with terms in this theme. Jesus does not "believe" people because he "knows" them (2:23–25). Jesus tells his disciples, "My food is to do the will of the one who sent me and to complete his work." "Doing" (Gk. *poieō*) and "completing" (Gr. *teleioō*) are responses of Jesus to the Father. Jesus' obedient actions are especially evident in John 5. For example, "the Son can do nothing from himself except what he *sees* the Father doing" (5:19). The Son "honors" (Gk. *timaō*) the Father (8:49), "knows" the Father and "keeps" (Gk. *tēreō*) his word (8:55). In John 17 Jesus "glorifies" and "knows" the Father.

As for all of the themes, the Believing theme is pervasive. The words included in this theme combined occur over a thousand times, with a majority of occurrences as part of the theme. As a result I will focus on key places that illustrate the breadth of the theme on the one hand and the development of theme on the other.

Jesus pointedly indicates that their belief (the verb "believed" is in the aorist or simple tense) needs to be confirmed by continuing in Jesus' word.

"AS MANY AS RECEIVED HIM"

The Prologue of John introduces the Believing theme, as one might expect, though all of chapter one serves this purpose. In the short paragraph devoted to John the Baptist, John tells us "He came as a witness to testify to the light, so that all might *believe* through him." The "light" here is the *Logos*, later identified as the only-begotten, and then Jesus Christ. John the Baptist came as a witness so that all might believe in that light. At the outset there is a universal intent with regard to the response, not limited to one particular group of people.

Nevertheless, the contrast between 1:10–11 and 1:12 quickly modifies the actual result of this universal purpose. On the one hand "He was in the world, and the world came into being through him; yet the world did not *know* him. He came to what was his own, and his own people did not *accept* him." John introduces two new terms for the theme: "know" (Gk. *ginōskō*) and "accept" (Gk. *lambanō*), both negated in this case. Here John gives a broad indication of the negative response which will appear in specific ways throughout the gospel. The world of humanity did not "know" him; that is, they had no recognition of him. Likewise, his own people did not "accept him," that is, even though Jesus was in their midst for all to see and hear, the Jewish people (and more specifically the Jewish leaders) refused to respond affirmatively to him.

The same term is used in the contrasting 1:12: "But to all who *received* him, who *believed* in his name, he gave power to become children of God." Notice that "received" is quickly defined as another term for "believe." Already we detect that the term "receive" (Gk. *lambanō*, translated as "accept" earlier) is used positively and negatively throughout the gospel with relation to responding to Jesus. Here in 1:12 there is a positive initiatory response and the result is that new birth as children of God comes about. In addition, one should notice that any positive response by humanity is only possible because of the grace of God; those who believe are "born from God" (1:13).

In the last section of the Prologue, John introduces one of the terms for "see" in the gospel, "And the Word became flesh and lived among us, and we have *seen* his glory, the glory as of the only-begotten of the Father, full of grace and truth." Throughout the gospel, John does use "see" in its physical sense (usually with Gk. *blepō*), but much more often uses "see" in the sense of spiritual sight (usually with Gk. *oraō* or *theaomai*, as here in 1:14). To "see" the glory of the *Logos* become flesh is to recognize that

God was fully present in the person of Jesus Christ, as 1:18 also clearly states. This "seeing" the glory of the *Logos* goes beyond the initial commitment of belief to a deeper understanding of who Jesus is.

Beyond the Prologue, John reintroduces John the Baptist and portrays him as the positive example of the Believing theme *par excellence*. Although John the Baptist tells the Pharisees that, "Among you stands one whom you do not know," when John *sees* Jesus coming to him (1:29), he says "Here is the Lamb of God who takes away the sin of the world!" In the paragraph comprising 1:29–34, John the Baptist exemplifies spiritual seeing (using all three Greek terms), knowing, and coming, that results in the confession of Jesus' identity as the "Son of God."

The remainder of John 1 focuses on the first disciples and abounds with the Believing theme. When John the Baptist repeats the phrase "*Look*, here is the Lamb of God" in 1:35, we are told, "The two disciples *heard* (Gk. *akouō*) him speaking and *followed* Jesus." Their literal hearing was also spiritual. In addition we detect that Jesus also has this spiritual sight in that he sees them following, asks "whom do you seek" and invites them to "*Come* (Gk. *erchomai*) and *see*." The disciples then "*came* and *saw* where he was staying and *remained* with him that day." Not only do we see an initiation of commitment, but the beginning of an on-going one in 1:40: "Andrew . . . was one of the two from John who *heard* and *followed* him." Andrew then brings Peter to Jesus. Further, Jesus finds Philip, and says "*follow* me," whereupon Philip tells Nathaniel "we have *found* (Gk. *euriskō*) the one whom Moses wrote of in the law and prophets." To Nathaniel's doubt, Philip responds, "*Come* and *see*." In response to Jesus' knowledge of Nathaniel, Nathaniel asks, "How do you *know* me?" then confesses upon Jesus' response, "Teacher, you are the Son of God, you are the King of Israel." As a result of this confession, John brings the introduction of the theme to a high point in the response of Jesus in 1:50–51: "Do you *believe* because I told you that I *saw* you under the fig tree? You will *see* greater things than these." And he said to him, "Very truly, I tell you, you will *see* heaven opened and the angels of God ascending and descending upon the Son of Man." Jesus promises Nathaniel that as a result of his placing of faith in Jesus, his spiritual sight would continue to develop.

The first chapter of John, then, not only sets out the broad framework of this theme in the Prologue with both its positive and negative trajectories, but in the stories of John the Baptist and the first disciples, the narrative establishes the positive trajectory with a range of expressions which will be reiterated and added to throughout the gospel.

TO BELIEVE OR NOT TO BELIEVE

Following the introduction in chapter one, the Believing theme largely develops in two blocks: chapters 2–12 and chapters 13–17. In 2–12 the emphasis in on initiation, though as noted previously, John considers an initial positive response no response at all if not maintained. To illustrate this position, John develops positive and negative trajectories where the negative result at times began as a positive initial response. John 13–17 emphasizes perseverance as Jesus prepares the disciples for his departure.

Examples of the purely positive trajectory of the Believing theme occur in the water to wine story (2:1–11), the encounter of Jesus and the Samaritan woman (4:4–24), and the healing of the royal official's son (4:46–54). The first and third of these examples are two of the miraculous signs that Jesus performs. As the chapter on the Signs theme shows, the Believing theme is often entwined with the signs.

In the first example, when Jesus performed the transformation of water to wine, John tells us, "Jesus did this, the first of his signs, in Cana of Galilee, and revealed his glory; and his disciples *believed* in him" (2:11).[3] Since the disciples had already responded to Jesus before, this notice is likely an example of a deeper level of believing. Indeed, this miracle may be a fulfillment of Jesus' promise to Nathaniel that he would "see greater things than these" (1:50). From this point onward John periodically states that the disciples "believed," suggesting that as they continued to follow Jesus, they also continued to reaffirm their commitment to Jesus as their understanding of him grew (see 2:22; 6:67–69; 11:14–16; 20:8; 20:26–29).

Later in his trip through Samaria, Jesus encounters a woman at Jacob's well and asks her for a drink of water (4:4–7). He answers the woman's confused reply with the hoped for positive response: "If you *knew* the gift of God, and who it is that is saying to you, 'Give me a drink,' you would have *asked* (Gk. *aiteō*) him, and he would have given you living water" (4:10). Notice that the Life theme is prominent in this passage

---

3. There is also a subtle ironic use of the theme in this miracle. In 2:8, John narrates that the steward did *not know* where the wine came from, but that the servant who drew the water *knew*.

(as is the Festival theme in the talk of Jacob's well and the correct place of worship). In her protestations to Jesus' answer, the woman shows that she is understanding *drink* (Gk. *pinō*) in a physical way (4:11–12). Jesus, however, is speaking on the spiritual level, so he says, "Everyone who *drinks* of this water will be thirsty again, but the one who *drinks* of the water that I will give him will never be thirsty." The language of response (i.e. *drinking)* is directly related to the circumstance of their location at the well. When Jesus goes on to tell the woman about her past, she responds with, "Sir, I *see* that you are a prophet" (4:19). Later she shows even more understanding: "I *know* that Messiah is coming (who is called Christ). When he comes, he will proclaim all things to us" (4:25). The woman's previous knowledge connects to her encounter with Jesus to produce greater understanding. Now the woman shows an authentic response by going to her town and urging the people to "*Come* and *see* a man who told me everything I have ever done!" (4:29). She is now inviting others to respond (like Andrew in chapter 1). The outcome as John narrates it in 4:39–42 is highly favorable: "Many *believed* in him;" "They *asked* him to *remain* with them;" "Many more *believed* because of his word." The end result was one of the most exalted confessions in the gospel: "They said to the woman, 'It is no longer because of what you said that we *believe*, for we have *heard* for ourselves, and we *know* that this one is truly the Savior of the world.'"

Outside of John 1, the story of the Samaritan woman and that of the royal official that follows, where the official and his household believe in Jesus, are the most intact positive examples of the Believing theme. John also gives some general notices of positive response in 10:42 and 12:11. In other instances, there is a combination of the positive with either ambiguous or negative response. An example of ambiguous response is the story of Nicodemus in 3:1–21. Nicodemus comes to Jesus with the words, "Rabbi, we *know* that you are a teacher who has come from God; for no one can do these signs that you do apart from the presence of God" (3:2). It becomes quickly evident that Nicodemus's knowledge is deficient. Further, Nicodemus fades from the narrative without making any type of response. Only later do we have some indication that Nicodemus might have responded in a positive way (7:50; 19:39). John also gives some generalized announcements of ambiguous response, such as in 2:23–24: "Many believed in his name because they saw the signs that he was doing. But Jesus on his part would not entrust himself to them, because he knew all people." Other seemingly positive but ambiguous responses include 6:14–15; 7:31, 40–44; 8:30–33; 11:45–46; and 12:42–43.

In contrast to the positive trajectory just outlined, throughout chapters 2–12, John also develops a negative trajectory of the theme as introduced in 1:10–11. Examples occur in 2:18–20; 5:10–47; 6:26–65; 7:19–48; 8:12–59; 9:13–41; 10:19–39; 11:47–57; 12:9–10. Each of the passages except the last two contains a dialogue/dispute between Jesus and various groups of Jews. In each instance, Jesus presents who he is and then calls on the listeners to believe in him. The result is almost uniformly a rejection of the call to believe. For instance, following the healing of the lame man in chapter 5, we read in 5:10–16 that the Jewish leaders were concerned that the miracle occurred on the Sabbath. As a result, "the Jews started persecuting Jesus, because he was doing such things on the Sabbath" (5:16). Already there is an indication of a likely negative response. This outcome develops through a distinctly pointed conversation between Jesus and the leaders introduced in 5:17–18, where Jesus claims certain prerogatives of God and the Jewish leaders then accuse him of claiming to be equal to God.[4] In the ensuing discourse, Jesus largely affirms their accusation, not because of his inherent identity, but because he is simply carrying out the wishes of his Father. This important discourse actually weaves together all seven themes. With regard to the Believing theme, Jesus first sets out who he is as carrying out the Father's desire of giving life and judging. Then Jesus declares in 5:22–23, "The Father judges no one but has given all judgment to the Son, so that all may *honor* (Gk. *timaō*) the Son just as they *honor* the Father. Anyone who does not *honor* the Son does not *honor* the Father who sent him." John juxtaposes the positive and the negative in parallel clauses using another verb of response, "honor." Jesus immediately defines what "honor" is in the following sentence: "Very truly, I tell you, anyone who *hears* my word and *believes* him who sent me has eternal life, and does not come under judgment, but has passed from death to life" (5:24). The call to the Jewish leaders is to hear and believe. The call is followed with the language of "hearing his voice" in 5:25 and 28.

In spite of Jesus' call to believe, the rest of the discourse implies unequivocally that the leaders reject his call. After setting out the witnesses of John the Baptist, Jesus' works (or signs), and the Father, Jesus

---

4. This passage is an important part of the Identity theme.

proclaims: "You have *never heard* [the Father's] voice or *seen* his form, and you do *not* have his word *abiding* in you, because you do *not believe* him whom he has sent" (5:38–39). He then reiterates with "I have come in my Father's name, and you do *not accept* me," and asks, "How can you *believe* when you *accept* glory from one another and do *not seek* the glory that comes from the one who alone is God?" (5:43–44). The final indictment comes when Jesus calls Moses as witness. He then punctuates their unbelief by the words, "If you *believed* Moses, you would *believe* me, for he wrote about me. But if you do *not believe* in his writings, how will you *believe* in my words?" (5:47).

In chapter 5, then, John narrates a clear illustration of the negative trajectory of the Believing theme. But notice how Jesus never revokes the call to believe. Indeed, later in chapter 12, John informs us that "Nevertheless many, even of the authorities, believed in him" (12:42). Even those who reject Jesus still have an open invitation to believe, no matter their current decision, though he makes clear that continuing unbelief leads to judgment (5:29). An examination of several of the instances of the negative trajectory confirms this open invitation, and none invalidate it.

We have already covered John 9 in some detail in the Life and Witness themes, but it is important to point out that this chapter is also remarkable for its side-by-side treatments of the positive and negative trajectories of the Believing theme. On the one hand the blind man whom Jesus heals develops spiritual sight throughout the story, as he must repeatedly confess what Jesus has done for him. As a result, there is a definitive positive response in 9:35–38: "[Jesus] said, "Do you *believe* in the Son of Man?" He answered, "And who is he, sir? Tell me, so that I may *believe* in him." Jesus said to him, "You have *seen* him, and the one speaking with you is he." He said, "Lord, I *believe*." And he *worshiped* (Gk. *proskyneō*) him." The initial belief of the healed blind man becomes an authentic, on-going commitment.

On the other hand, the authorities, when confronted with the evidence of what Jesus did, do not believe. At the end of John 9 Jesus confronts them with the words, "I came into this world for judgment so that those who do *not see* may *see*, and those who *do see* may become blind" (9:39). In response, "Some of the Pharisees who were with him heard these things and said to him, 'We are not blind, are we?' Jesus said to them, 'If you were blind, you would not have sin. But since you say,

'We see,' your sin remains'" (9:40–41). What is surprising here is that the Pharisees appear to be quite aware of what Jesus is telling them, but refuse to consider the possibility that what he says is true.

I have only pointed to a small portion of the Believing theme in the first half of John, but hopefully in such a way that you are now able to detect and interpret the theme in its many other occurrences.

KEEP ON KEEPING ON

In the second half of John, the initiation aspect of this theme recedes to the background. The emphasis instead is on the persistence and depth of believing. Especially in John 13–17, we see a shift in the vocabulary for this theme. Now the emphasis is on knowing, following, seeing and remaining as well as the affirmation that the disciples already believe (with the exception of Judas Iscariot). When the disciples have questions or requests, as in 13:37, 14:5, 8, and 22, Jesus does not respond to them as those who do not know or believe, but as those who need to deepen their understanding.

Two essentially new verbs are added to the theme in these chapters: "love" (Gk. *agapaō*) and "keep." In 13:31, after the departure of Judas Iscariot, Jesus says, "A new commandment I give to you, that you should *love* one another, just as I have loved you." He continues in 14:15: "If you *love* me, you will *keep* my commandments." Jesus reiterates this combination of love and keep in 14:21, 23 and 15:10. Thus loving and keeping along with remaining now become the focal points of the Believing theme. The three verbs are all concerned with persevering in the faith.

These three terms come together in a forceful way in 15:1–17. Jesus uses the "parable" of the vine and branches to convey the necessity of staying intimately connected to him. The verb "remain" is repeated eleven times, usually as an imperative (a request/command) or in a conditional statement ("if you remain . . ."). Jesus urges his disciples to stay the course in their faith. As a result they will "bear much fruit" (9:5, cf. 9:2). What does this "remaining" entail? Jesus brings the parable to more specificity in 15:9b–10: "*remain* in my love. If you *keep* my commandments, you will *remain* in my love, just as I have *kept* my Father's commandments and *remain* in his love." Jesus then repeats that the commandment is to "love one another, just as I have loved you" (15:12). There is an element of circularity in this passage, but the intent is that there is no distinction between "remaining," "loving" and "keeping." Believing in Jesus is a dynamic, growing and persistent process that shows itself through "bearing fruit."

In this second half of John, the positive trajectory is emphasized, though at points there are intrusions of the negative. Immediately following the previous section, Jesus in 15:18–25 highlights the world's ongoing rejection of him and by extension the disciples. He uses the term "hate," the very opposite of love. Despite the fact that people saw all that Jesus did, they continue to hate him and persecute him.

John concludes his gospel with a strong emphasis on the Believing theme. In chapter 20 when Peter and the Beloved Disciple ran to the tomb, the gospel writer tells us that the Beloved Disciple "*saw* and *believed*, for they had not yet *understood* (Gk. *oida*) the scripture that he must rise from the dead" (20:8–9). This is not initial belief but belief in the resurrection. Mary Magdalene tells the disciples, "I have *seen* the Lord" (20:18).

This positive belief in the resurrection has its negative counterpart in the person of Thomas, who in 20:25 refuses to believe apart from eyewitness proof that Jesus is alive: "unless I *see* . . . I will not *believe.*" This demand for eyewitness proof provides the context for Jesus' last statement on the subject. After Thomas does see Jesus and confesses "My Lord and my God!" Jesus states, "Have you believed me because you have seen me? Blessed are those who have not *seen* and yet *believe*" (20:29). In relaying this encounter, John prepares the way for those who will hear the gospel later: will they hear and then believe or reject the testimony of those who have believed?

CONCLUSION

The Believing theme is the most widely disseminated theme in the gospel, occurring in some form in every chapter. As with all the themes, one cannot isolate the Believing theme from its interaction with the other themes. All of the various terms used in this theme occur in contexts that show a response to Jesus as he is revealed in other themes. In every case where the Believing theme appears, another theme occurs alongside it, whether Identity, Life, Festival, Witness, Signs, or Destiny. The practical reason is that verbs demanding (or at least implying) an object primarily compose this theme. Even verbs such as "come," when part of the theme, imply a destination that belongs to another theme (e.g. 1:39, 46; 3:20). A person "believes" in Jesus, "drinks" living water, "eats" the Bread of

Life, "follows" the Messiah, "honors" the Father, "obeys" his command-ments, "remains" in the vine, "listens to" his voice, "knows" the truth. It is imperative then, that the student of the Believing theme always un-derstands the object of believing in John: Jesus Christ, the Only Son of the Father, the Way, Truth, and Life, who poured out "water and blood" on the cross. Apart from Jesus Christ as object of believing, believing itself (and the concept of truth) becomes untethered and is susceptible to attach to any object. Faith itself becomes the object of faith and the common notion of "If you only believe (something)" is the result.

6

Signs

"**W**HAT SIGN WILL YOU do that we might see and believe you?" This strange question follows the feeding of the 5000 and comes from those who were actually fed. The question imbeds a great irony in John; many who witness a miracle of Jesus do not recognize that the miracle is intended to point to Jesus as the life-giving savior. Instead they keep asking for more. The irony is at the heart of the Signs theme.

One of the most noted characteristics of the Gospel of John is the identification of Jesus' miraculous deeds as "signs." In the Synoptic Gospels these acts are routinely designated as miracles. But John, while not playing down the miraculous nature of various acts such as the turning water to wine, the various healings and the feeding of the 5000, focuses not on the deeds themselves but their significance as testimonies to the identity of Jesus. In contrast to the numerous miracles recorded in the Matthew, Mark, and Luke, John only includes a select number of signs, but tells us that there were many others (20:30). And John tells us why: "these things are written so that you might believe that Jesus is the Christ, the Son of God and that believing you might have life in his name" (20:31). In that key purpose statement, we see that the Signs theme is very closely aligned with the Believing theme as well as others.

A pertinent question at the outset is whether the Signs theme is a theme at all rather than a motif. As we will see, the Signs theme goes far beyond the well-known seven or eight signs. The term "sign" (Gk. *sēmeia*) occurs in quite a few other contexts in John, as well as the related term "work" (Gk. *ergon*). The theme has less to do with the signs themselves and much more to do with whom the signs point to (Jesus) and especially with people's response to the signs. The signs serve the purpose of separating out those who believe from those who do not as the prologue already indicates (1:10–12). The response of individuals (or groups) to the signs is varied from full belief to questioning belief to outright hostility. So the Signs theme has a great deal to do with the relationship between an act of Jesus and the perceptions of different people on the nature and significance of the act. In fact, what one finds throughout John is that the signs are usually only the precipitating factor leading to a discussion of who Jesus is. Further, a deeper investigation of each sign that John details will show that he builds a symbolic level of meaning into the narration of each sign. The symbolism inevitably connects with one of the other themes, especially those related to the identity of Jesus (Identity, Life, Festival).

"HE REVEALED HIS GLORY . . ."

John subtly introduces the Signs theme in chapter 1, but only in hindsight is this introduction evident. So to initiate the discussion, I want to look carefully at the conclusion to the first named sign, the water to wine story. John 2:1–10 is a well-told anecdote about Jesus' first miracle at a wedding in Cana of Galilee that he accomplished at the behest of his mother. The story itself has a great deal of symbolism, especially related to the Festival theme and the Destiny motif of Jesus' "hour." But verse 11 is where our interests lie: "Jesus performed this first of the signs in Cana of Galilee and he revealed his glory and his disciples believed in him."

John emphasizes three key elements related to the Signs theme in his interpretive statement. First, there will be other acts of Jesus designated as signs. Actually the only other miracle designated specifically this way is the healing of the royal official's son in John 4. But the miraculous elements in the healing of the lame man in John 5, the feeding of the five thousand and Jesus' walking on water in John 6, the healing of the blind man in John 9 and the raising of Lazarus in John 11, all correspond to John's idea of a sign (some also add the miraculous catch of fish in John 21), and often the term for sign or work appears in the subsequent material.

Second, John tells us in 2:11 that Jesus revealed his glory. In this short phrase, John gives the importance of the sign; it shows who Jesus is. In this respect the signs could be categorized under the meta-theme of Revelation. In using this language of revealing his glory, John is recalling the notice of the incarnation in 1:14, "and the word became flesh and dwelt among us and we beheld his glory." The greatest sign for John is indeed the incarnation (which encompasses Jesus' life, death, and resurrection). By extension, all of the signs in the gospel reveal something of

Jesus' glory and John wants the reader to look beyond the miracle itself to what is says about that glory.

The third key element of the interpretive statement in 2:11 is that "his disciples believed in him." Here John indicates the proper response to the revealing of Jesus' glory in the sign, believing. As I have previously observed, the Signs theme is closely connected with the Believing theme in that the signs of Jesus are intended to elicit a response of believing. What we quickly discover by the end of John 2 is that the signs do not always elicit the proper response; many times people respond with quasi-belief or unbelief. This third element once again helps us to reinterpret something John has already said in chapter one. When Jesus saw Nathaniel under the fig tree and called him a guileless Israelite, Nathaniel responded with a confession of Jesus' identity, to which Jesus replied, "Because I said that I saw you under the fig tree, do you believe?" In this incident we have what appears to be a supernatural assessment of character by Jesus and a response of belief by Nathaniel. Together with the water to wine sign that follows, John gives us ideal models for the proper response to Jesus' signs.

With these three elements in mind, the tracing of the signs theme takes on a much more complex dimension in that there are a number of other incidents in the gospel which function in the same way as the miraculous signs, but are not of the same miraculous character. In addition, when actually looking for the Signs theme in the text of John, John does not develop the theme in the miraculous signs themselves but subsequent to the events.

Simply moving to the next story in chapter 2 illustrates this thesis. When Jesus and his disciples go to Jerusalem for the Passover in 2:13, he then enters the temple and causes havoc by freeing the sacrificial animals and overturning the tables of the moneychangers. The response of the Jewish leaders uses "signs" language in 2:18: "What sign can you show us for doing this thing?" In their response, the Jewish leaders show that they have missed the sign itself regarding Jesus' symbolic destruction of the temple (Festival theme). In replying, "Destroy this temple and in three days I will raise it up" (2:19), Jesus interprets what he has done in the cleansing of the temple episode as a replacement of the temple in himself, and points toward the passion and resurrection as the ultimate sign relating to his replacement of the temple. This very saying then becomes a type of sign which John then interprets for the reader in

2:21–22. Thus in chapter 2 we see a miracle of Jesus, an action of Jesus, and a saying of Jesus that all function as signs.

John does not tell us if the Jewish leaders responded with belief or not, though chapter 5 and 7 would indicate not. He does tell us in 2:23, however, that, "many believed in his name because they saw the signs that he was doing." The response would appear to be the proper one, except for the notice that follows: "But Jesus on his part would not entrust himself to them, because he knew all people . . . for he himself knew what was in a person." So within chapter two John has indicated the full range of responses to Jesus' signs from full faith to ambiguous faith to the leaders' apparent lack of faith. Notice also that John says the people in Jerusalem saw the "signs he was doing." John does not detail those signs unless he is referring to the temple cleansing. More likely Jesus was performing miraculous deeds that John leaves out from his story.

Although there is some minor development of the theme in the story of the Samaritan woman (4:29: "Come and see a man who told me everything I have ever done! He cannot be the Messiah, can he?"), the healing of the royal official's son in 4:46–54 is where John next explores the theme. This miracle is in fact the only one in which John develops the Signs theme within the telling of the sign story itself. When the royal official comes to Jesus asking to heal his son, Jesus responds: "Unless you see signs and wonders you will not believe." Jesus provokes the man with a key observation regarding the relation between "signs and wonders" and faith. Jesus implies that unless a miraculous event is present then for some faith will never happen. A further implication explored later in chapter 6 is that even if a sign leads to "faith," is that faith a true faith in Jesus or simply a shallow response to the miracle? In this particular instance, the royal official continues to press Jesus to heal his son and when Jesus speaks "Go, your son lives," we are told, "the man believed the word which Jesus spoke to him and left" (4:50). Thus John signifies that the man's faith is more than based on the sign alone, but on Jesus himself. Note that this sign also develops the themes of Life and Believing.

In contrast to the positive result of the sign in the healing of the royal official's son, the response to the healing of the lame man in 5:1–9 is anything but positive. Symbolically, John relates the event to the Festival theme ("a feast of the Jews" in 5:1 and Sabbath in 5:9–10) and to the Life theme in the actual healing. The leaders do not see the sign positively, though, because Jesus performed it on the Sabbath. They refused to believe because the deed conflicted with their doctrine. John uses this conflict to lead into a discussion of Jesus prerogative to heal on the Sabbath, a debate that encompasses all of the themes discussed in this book. The Signs theme appears in Jesus' roll call of witnesses to himself in 5:31–40: John the Baptist, Jesus "works", his Father, and the scriptures. In 5:36 Jesus refers to his works: "But I have a testimony greater than John's. The works that the Father has given me to complete, the very works that I am doing, testify on my behalf that the Father has sent me." The signs or "works" of Jesus then are part of the evidence for who he is claiming to be. John 10:25–39 extends this concept to a much greater degree.

John 6 continues to expand the Signs theme by narrating two signs, indicating apparent authentic belief on the basis of the sign and then exploring whether or not the surface confession is actually true. The first of two miraculous events in this chapter is the feeding of the 5000, the only miracle included in all four gospel accounts. The miracle itself is properly interpreted as relating to the Life theme and the Festival theme (in its stated proximity to Passover). Not until after the miracle does the Signs theme come to prominence in 6:14–15: "When the people saw the sign that he had done, they began to say, 'This is indeed the Prophet coming into the world.' When Jesus realized that they were about to come and take him by force to make him king, he withdrew again to the mountain by himself."

We have what appears to be a true confession of belief, but Jesus realizes that the confession is an earthly and political one rather than one that truly recognizes and confesses his identity. Jesus' perception of the people's misguided understanding leads to the conversation with the people in Capernaum after the miracle of walking on water is narrated, a "sign" that focuses on the Identity theme. When the people find Jesus in Capernaum, Jesus says to them, "Truly, truly, I tell you, you are looking for me, not because you saw signs, but because you ate your fill of the loaves" (6:26). By his words, Jesus is actually separating the miracle ("you ate from the bread and were filled") from the "sign", that is, the miracle as a symbolic picture of Jesus as the source and giver of life. The crowd's total lack of understanding is evident in their further response in 6:30: "So they said to him, "What sign are you going to give us then, so that we may see it and believe you? What work are you performing?" In the ensuing "Bread of Life" discourse with its increasingly predestinarian language and graphic "eating and drinking of body and blood" language, the end result is that many who had professed belief left from following Jesus. The faith based on signs proved to be ephemeral except for his true disciples.

Though the Signs theme continues more or less along these lines in John 7 (cf. 7:3–4, 21–24, 31), it is in chapter 9 that John dramatically illustrates the bifurcation of belief and unbelief in the aftermath of a sign. The sign itself, the healing of the blind man in 9:1–7, is once again told in a way that focuses on other themes, in this case Identity and Life. The remainder of the chapter also develops the themes of Festival, Witness, and Believing. However, the Signs theme is the foundation of the chapter. At every instance where someone is called to testify, the sign itself is recited, either as a question or as an answer. One is left to wonder whether the neighbors or the parents develop faith, but in the encounter of the healed man and the Pharisees, we see two phenomena. For the man, as he repeatedly testifies to the sign his faith increases. Ultimately he confesses and worships Jesus (9:35–38). The Pharisees on the other hand, refuse to accept the sign as valid even in the face of overwhelming evidence. Their predisposition toward not believing leads to "blindness" on their part (cf. 9:39–41). So we see that the sign itself, though clearly pointing to the identity of Jesus, is not sufficient in itself to engender belief. John explores this insufficiency in chapter 10 during Hanukkah. In response to a question about Jesus' identity as the Messiah, Jesus responds in 10:25 with "I told you and you do not believe; the works which I do in the name of my Father, these witness about me, but you do not believe because you are not my sheep." When the Jewish leaders took up stones to stone him, Jesus rejoindered, "Many good works I have shown you from my Father; for which are you stoning me?" and a few verses later: "if I don't do the works of my Father, don't believe me, but if I do them, even if you don't believe me, believe the works, so that you might know and understand that I the Father is in me and I in the Father" (10:38). The immediate result is that "they sought to seize him again" (10:39).

While signs may lead to full faith in the One doing them, without a predisposition to belief, unbelief and even hostility may result. The same pattern seen in chapters 9 and 10 holds for the chapter 11 sign, the raising of Lazarus. The sign itself, though spectacular, may build faith for those who are open (cf. 11:37, 45; also 12:9, 18), but certainly does not ensure faith, especially to those who are hostile to Jesus (cf. 11:46–53 and 12:11, 19). We will not treat this sign here since the emphasis is largely on the Identity, Life, Believing, and Destiny themes. I treat the sign in more detail in the Life theme chapter.

Many commentators have labeled the first half of John (usually 1:19–12:50) as "The Book of Signs." There is ample reason for this designation; not only do all of the miraculous events occur in these chapters, save for the resurrection and the catch of fish in chapter 21, but the theme largely concludes by chapter 12. In only one notice in 15:24 and in the Thomas story of John 20, along with the closing purpose statement in 20:30–31, do we have any further expansion. The conclusion of the Signs theme in chapter 12 is primarily a negative one: "Although he had performed so many signs in their presence, they did not believe in him" (12:37). The crowd, who had come to Jesus because they had heard about the raising of Lazarus in 12:18, continued to question who he was in 12:34–36. John interprets their questioning as unbelief and draws on Isaiah 53:1 and 6:10 to explain the lack of response. Some did believe, but even then their belief was questionable because they were afraid to confess that belief (12:42–43).

SIGNS FAITH?

John places a great deal of emphasis on the signs and works of Jesus as indicators of who he was and what he came to do. But in retrospect, John demonstrates that "signs faith," or a belief based only on a sign, is no faith at all if it is not developed through a continued relationship and trust in Jesus, such as illustrated by the royal official and the healed blind man. Those who were simply looking for outward miracles or who were hostile to Jesus could and did dispute or deny the signs that pointed to Jesus. The true disciple, however, recognizes that the sign is an indicator of Jesus' glory and thus true believing results (2:11; 6:67–69). Even the story of Thomas in 20:24–29 is illustrative of this point. Thomas, despite the fact he had been with Jesus throughout, was still partly at the level of "signs faith" in that he needed to see physical evidence of the resurrection. Nonetheless, when he saw the resurrected Jesus, he did recognize his glory and worshiped him as "my Lord and my God."

Ultimately, the Signs theme is a theme of differentiation. In the declaration of purpose in 20:30–31, John gives the reason for the signs; they point to Jesus with the hope that they will engender faith. There is actually an enigmatic textual dilemma in 20:31. The verb for "believe,"

Gk. *pisteuō*, has two almost equally attested tense forms in the ancient manuscripts which yield slightly different meanings. The aorist form of the verb likely places the emphasis on the beginning of the action with an appropriate translation of "so that you might come to believe." Here the emphasis is placed on the signs for an evangelistic goal. Other manuscripts contain the present tense, with an emphasis on on-going action, thus "so you might continue to believe." In this case, John's purpose for the signs would be growth in faith, not necessarily the initiation of faith. The evidence is so close for either reading that a firm decision is not possible. A consideration of the Signs theme in the gospel, however, places greater weight on the discipleship aspect in that rarely did a sign of Jesus actually serve to initiate faith that continued to grow. Instead, the signs served to bolster the faith of those who had already shown a disposition to faith. Both for John's day and our day, miraculous signs may function as an entry to faith, but usually only in conjunction with other factors.

THE CROSS AS SIGN

The cross and resurrection is *the* sign in John. The total event is called Jesus' "glorification." On the cross Jesus completes the work he was sent to accomplish. In the resurrection Jesus is shown to be everything the gospel has said he was. The cross and resurrection as sign appears as early as John 2. After the clearing of the temple, the Jewish leaders ask, "what sign will you carry out [to show your authority] to do these things?" "Destroy this temple and in three days I will raise it up," Jesus responds. We obviously have a Festival theme image here in Jesus' fulfillment/replacement of the Temple, but the very basis for this image relies on the ultimate sign, the cross and resurrection. The cross as Sign points to Life, desires Believing, and fulfills Jesus' destiny so that our destiny can change. Perhaps the key location of this "signifying" role is John 3:14 where Jesus' "lifting up" (as Son of Man) is compared to Moses' lifting up of the serpent in the wilderness. Immediately after the statement, we have the interpretation, "so that all who believe in him might have eternal life" (3:15). But just as it took gazing upon the serpent to bring about healing in the wilderness, so one must gaze at the One on the cross to receive eternal life. The sign of the cross points to God's love in that God "gave his only Son." John cleverly speaks of the cross as "sign" again in John 12, where after Jesus states that if he "is lifted up from the earth, I will draw all people to myself," John comments that Jesus "signified"

(Gk. *sēmaino*) what kind of death he would die (12:33). Ironically the sign of the cross was perpetrated through the designs of the very people Jesus came to save, though the sign also fulfilled scripture within the plan of God (18:30–32). Pilate made the sign even clearer by placing a "sign" (Gk. *titlon*) on the cross in three languages stating that Jesus was King of the Jews.

CONCLUSION

The Signs theme is an uneasy theme. In an age where scientific fact is the purported basis for whatever faith many people may have, the Signs theme shows that even in the face of certain events, people actually choose to believe what they want to believe. Ultimately, reason alone is not enough. People must look beyond the event to the Person who gives meaning to the event. This contention is no less true today than the day John wrote, "Jesus did many other signs . . . but these are written that you might believe."

7

Destiny

"**A**RE THERE NOT TWELVE hours in the day?" Jesus asks his disciples in 11:9. In this question Jesus is expressing the reality that time is limited and that time is significant. Most of us ask ourselves (or others!) "What time is it?" many times each day. Time is one way we measure our lives. For John, time was of eternal importance. His answer to the question "What time is it?" was "it is time to put your trust in Jesus Christ." For John, how you act now determines your future and your future affects the quality of your life now.

Our final theme, the Destiny theme, is arguably the most difficult both in its identification throughout the text of John and in its theological implications. The Destiny theme includes the thread of John's gospel dealing with eschatology. Some scholars see little evidence of traditional "future" eschatology in John, preferring the phrase "realized eschatology." But in fact, John has much to say about the future of humans. There are clear statements in John about resurrection to life and to judgment. Some scholars have sought to explain away such future eschatology as the work of later editors rather than the evangelist. An understanding of the Destiny theme, however, brings together both "realized" and "future" eschatology into a continuum rather than two separate trains of thinking. I prefer the phrase "continuous eschatology."

A distinctive factor in this continuum is the use of time in the gospel. Throughout the text, time is noted, ranging from the seemingly mundane like the time of day to the symbolic as in "the hour" motif. Indeed, with "the hour" motif, we discover that John presents Jesus himself as part of the Destiny theme. Jesus' own destiny is absolutely significant for the destiny of others.

The heart of the Destiny theme is the interaction between the love of God for humanity and how that love is experienced, both in the present and the future. Throughout the gospel, those who respond positively to God's giving of the Son, experience God's love as eternal life. Those who reject the gift experience God's love as judgment. The love of God encompasses both. In John 3, it becomes apparent that apart from believing in the one whom God sent, the world lies in judgment. God loves the world, but that same world rejects God.

A complicating factor in this theme is the relationship of choice and predestination. Throughout the gospel, people are called on to believe and follow Jesus Christ. There is a seeming choice to follow that call or to reject it. On the other hand, there are multiple instances of what appears to be deterministic language, the language of God's drawing or choosing those who believe. The uncomfortable question then becomes, is a person's destiny a free choice or a predestined reality? Any answer to this question must take the Destiny theme into account as it plays out in the gospel in conjunction with the other themes.

Ultimately, the conclusions of studying this theme may appear ambiguous, leaving more questions than answers. So too, though the topic of judgment is unpalatable to many, judgment is a distinct reality in the theology of John's gospel and must be clearly identified and interpreted. Although judgment may be disconcerting on the one hand, the understanding of God's infinite love is assuring. Despite the seeming ambiguity or unpalatability of issues in the Destiny theme, John pushes the reader to think deeply about the present state of our existence with relation to the future. Further, John anchors the destiny of the world to the destiny of Jesus, whose "hour" on the cross opened the door for a new destiny for that world.

As with the other themes, John introduces Destiny in the Prologue. Already in the Prologue a tension exists between the *Logos* as the "light of men" and the darkness that does not comprehend it (1:5). John writes in symbolic language that he develops later in chapter 3, where the Destiny theme is most clearly and prominently set out. In 1:9–11 the tension rises between the light coming into the world and that same world that does not know the light; even his own people do not receive him. In the Prologue, the readers cannot yet discern the implications of the world's rejection, but they do know one outcome of those who receive the light—they become children of God (1:12–13). This designation is arguably related to the Identity theme, but points to the Destiny of eternal life.

Beyond the Prologue, Destiny is mainly in the background until John 3, aside from the time motif. The one occurrence of the theme is implied. When John the Baptist declares, "Behold, the Lamb of God who takes away the sin of the world," he connects the world of humanity with the concept of sin. Along with "the world", "sin" (Gk. *hamartia*) is another motif of the Destiny theme throughout the gospel. Sin is connected in John with death, which results from unbelief in Jesus (so 8:24, "If you do not believe that I am, you will die in your sins"). The implication is that the future of the unbelieving world is death and not eternal life, while the action of the "Lamb of God" changes this future (see Festival theme).

TIME AND THE HOUR OF THE CROSS

Time is also an element first evident in the Prologue, not as eschatology but as protology, not as specific time, but significant time. The "In the beginning" of 1:1 sets the entirety of the gospel in the setting of eternal time so that the events of the gospel narrative proper are only a point in time within the eternality of God's existence. John the Baptist reiterates this reality in his statement: "One is coming after me is more important than me because he existed before me" (1:15, repeated in 1:30). Throughout the gospel, John reminds the reader of this eternality in various words of Jesus related to his Identity (for example, 3:13, 6:38; 8:23, 58).

Time becomes specific in 1:14, "And the Word became flesh . . ." Whatever the form of the Word implied before 1:14, that very Word becomes part of the space-time reality of humanity in 1:14. The rest of the gospel narrative relates events in this time-space reality. John never lets the reader forget time; indeed he indicates time in numerous ways ranging from the seemingly insignificant or mundane to highly symbolic. Beginning in 1:29, John often uses progressive markers of time, such as "the next day" (Gk. *epaurion;* 1:29, 35, 43). He also gives the hour of the day that certain events occur, such as "the tenth hour" (1:39, see also 4:6; 19:14) or nighttime (3:1; 13:30). Several times Jesus contrasts day and night (9:4–5; 11:9–10). John indicates time of year by reference to the Jewish festivals.

The most important marker of time is not the identification of a time of day, or a particular day or year, but the appointed "hour" (Gk. *hōra*) of Jesus "glorification." This "hour" appears almost off-handedly in the miracle at Cana (2:4), but even in this instance, Jesus' action of turning water to wine becomes significant for Johannine symbolism (see

Festival theme). The notices that Jesus' hour "had not yet come" (7:30; 8:20), and Jesus' remarks similar to "the hour is coming" (4:21, 23; 5:25, 28), point to a future moment of consummation when Jesus would complete what he had come to do. Jesus' appointed hour was his crucifixion. By the use of the "hour" motif, John leads the reader to the inexorable conclusion of Jesus' time among humanity. In 12:23, 27 and 17:1, Jesus speaks of the hour as having arrived and John reiterates this conclusion in 13:1.

As to what the "hour" entails, we see two key terms put together in the space of a few verses, "glorify" and "lift up." First, when the "Greeks" come, Jesus responds that, "the hour has come for the Son of Man to be glorified" (12:23). Then in what is likely the counterpart to the prayer in Gethsemane, Jesus prays in 12:27, "now my soul is distress, and what should I pray. Father, save me from this hour? But because of this, I came for this hour. Father, glorify your name." Now is the moment for Jesus time on earth to be consummated and thus to "glorify" the Father on the cross. That the cross is intended comes clearly in 12:32: "and if I am lifted up from the earth (cf. 3:13), I will draw all people to myself." John adds that he used "lifted up" to show the kind of death he would die, namely crucifixion. At the cross, Jesus would complete what the Father destined him to do. In the final words on the cross, "it is finished," Jesus sums up the hour of his destiny to reveal the Father to the world and to bring salvation to that same world.

Before any other consideration of the Destiny theme, we must understand that Jesus Christ is an anchor of the theme in an essential way. Jesus' "hour" is the key to the destiny of humanity. In Jesus' fulfillment of the hour, people have the opportunity to fulfill their own destiny to eternal life. Likewise, those who reject Jesus' hour, remain destined to judgment.

LOVE AND THE WORLD

The weightiest expression of the Destiny theme takes place in John 3:16–21. Here John works together a combination of God's love and the eschatological outcomes of eternal life or judgment. In the Destiny theme John joins Revelation and Response closely together.

The bedrock of the Destiny theme is God's love for the world as stated in the first words of John 3:16, "For God so loved the world." This statement is unqualified in its scope with respect to the world, deserving or not. God simply loves the world no matter what. But what exactly does John mean by God's "love" and "the world"? Many who have memorized John 3:16 and perhaps quoted it many times, might think the terms are self-evident, but as many of my students over the years have discovered, there is more here than meets the eye.

The verb "love" (Gk. *agapaō*) is common throughout the New Testament and relatively so in John. Like so many other words, however, the specific nuance depends on the context. Thus, love in the gospel may properly fit with several other themes. At its core, love is the expression of a positive bond of affection between personal beings or between a person and a non-personal entity. In John, the Father loves the Son (3:35; 10:17; 17:24, 26) and the Son loves the Father (14:31). This eternal bond of affection between persons of the Godhead fits into the Identity theme.

Jesus develops a distinct bond of love with his disciples (13:1; 13:34). There is a special affection expressed between Jesus and Mary, Martha, Lazarus (11:5) and "the disciple whom Jesus loved" (13:23; see Witness theme). This bond is the normal one between friends. These friends are those who have responded to Jesus (Believing theme). Jesus encourages his disciples to show their love by keeping his commandments, particularly "to love one another" (13:34; 15:12, 17).

In John 3:16–21, however, we see two other nuances to love. First, God "loves" the world. As the ensuing discussion will indicate, "world" represents humanity as a whole, who are largely against God. God's love as expressed here is absolute charity, an affection given without deserts— a love given in spite of the possibility and even probability of rejection. As confirmation of this reality, John in the second nuance tells us in 3:19 that, "people loved the darkness rather than the light." A similar use is found in 12:43, "[the Pharisees] loved the glory of men rather than the glory of God." This "love" is not affection between persons or for God, but for a misplaced object, in these cases darkness and the glory of men.

The "world" (Gk. *kosmos*) as John understands it here is the entirety of humanity. *Kosmos* occurs more frequently in this gospel than any other NT document save 1 John, where it occurs twice as often. Together John and 1 John contain more occurrences of *kosmos* than the rest of the NT combined. It is not surprising then that the term has a range of meanings, just as "world" does in English. *Kosmos* in John can refer to the created order (1:10; 17:5, 24) or the planet we live on (11:9; 12:25). *Kosmos* as the earth is often set in contrast to heaven in a type of spatial dualism, such as the number of references to Jesus "coming into the world," or the Father sending Jesus into the world. Jesus states in stark terms, "You are from this world, I am not from this world" (8:23). Likewise, Jesus says to Pilate, "my kingdom is not from this world" (18:36).

Implied in each of these uses is the *kosmos* as representing human-ity, as is the case in most of John.[1] In many instances *kosmos* as humanity appears to be simply neutral as in "God so loved the world," Jesus as "Savior of the world," or as "the one who comes from heaven and gives life to the world." We might even be tempted to see these as positive references to humanity as being the objects of God's love. That God does reach out to the world in Jesus is positive, but the world of humanity as a whole stands in opposition to God almost from the beginning of the gospel and numerous times throughout. God's love for the world and Jesus' coming to save the world are indicative of a condition that needs to be changed. And in fact, the world of humanity "loves the darkness rather than the light" (3:19) and "hates" Jesus (7:7) and his followers (15:18–19). The world is ruled by the devil, "the ruler of this world" (12:31; 14:30; 16:11).

While one could argue that *kosmos* in John 3:16 refers to a more encompassing view for the world as the entirety of the cosmos or the physical earth with all living creatures, as the gospel proceeds it is clear that John is thinking primarily of thinking, feeling, willing men and women (cf. 1:29; 4:42). Some have argued that "world" in John 3:16 in-cludes only the "elect." The use of the term in the rest of the gospel shows that argument to be totally false. By and large John portrays the world as arrayed against God and the one he sent, Jesus, as well as against his fol-lowers. This portrayal is evident almost immediately in the succeeding verses in John 3:17–21. The world needs God's salvation (3:17), and even though "the light has come into the world," "people loved the darkness rather than the light" (3:19).

God's unqualified love for the world results in the gift of his Son, so that "everyone who believes in him might . . . have eternal life." John 3:17 reiterates this intention: "For God sent his Son into the world . . . so

---

1. Notice the identification of the world with humans in John 3:19, "This is the judg-ment, that the light has come into *the world*, and *people* loved the darkness rather than the light."

that the world might be saved through him." Here we have a crossover of the Destiny and Life themes. The letter of First John confirms the universality of the scope of God's love in Johannine thought. There the author proclaims, "God is love." Love is the dominant characteristic of God (1 John 4). God's loving action in the sending of his Son as an "atoning sacrifice" (Gk. *ilasmos)* was "not for our [sins] only, but for the whole world" (1 John 2:2).

Is John 3:16 the only place where the gospel speaks of God's unqualified love for the world? In the actual terms, yes, but the concept of God's love for the world is evident throughout John. In those places where Jesus is referred to as bringing salvation to the world, we see a reiteration of the love introduced in 3:16. God sent his son "so that the world might be saved through him" (3:17; cf. 12:47). Jesus is "Savior of the world" (4:42). He is the one "who gives life to the world" (6:33) and "gives [his] flesh for the life of the world" (6:51). He is the "light of the world" who gives the "light of life" (8:12; cf. 12:46).

The Gospel of John does not just speak of God's love for the world, but shows that love. I am not referring here to the passion, though the passion, death and resurrection are indeed the pinnacle of God's loving action. What I refer to are the words and actions of Jesus throughout the gospel as expressions of God's love. In John's view, every word that Jesus speaks and every action that Jesus takes is a word of love or an action of love intended to bring salvation to the world. When we examine the gospel with this viewpoint, we must reassess various sections of the gospel. This principle is particularly true of those passages where Jesus is in conflict with those with whom he is speaking, but also applies with every interaction that Jesus has.

LOVE, LIFE AND JUDGMENT

If one takes God's unqualified love for the world as absolute in its effects, it might lead to a universalistic view of salvation whereupon all are saved period. This view is not John's. God's absolute love does not result in a universal salvation or in a fully positive response from humanity. John makes it clear that there are two basic responses, believing and unbelieving, and two corresponding outcomes, eternal life and judgment. The Believing theme, of course, delves into the responses, while the Destiny theme is concerned with the outcomes.

As one initial example, consider the conclusion of John 9 follow-ing the positive response of the healed blind man. Jesus remarks, "I came into the world for judgment, so that those who don't see might see and those who see might become blind." The Pharisees take Jesus to be speaking to them and ask, "We are not blind, are we?" Jesus answers with a pronouncement that connects the contrasting pairs of blindness/sight with sin/no sin: "If you were blind you would have no sin; but now that you say, 'We see,' your sin remains." Jesus is speaking of spiritual sight and spiritual blindness.

These two outcomes correspond to the eschatological destinies of eternal life and judgment. Throughout John these two destinies are re-peated over and over both as pairs and alone. When Jesus tells Nicodemus that no one can see or enter the kingdom of God unless that person is born again, the implications of both not entering or entering are present. This entrance to the "kingdom of God" takes on John's particular cast when the phrase becomes "eternal life" in 3:15 and thereafter in the gos-pel. "Eternal life" (Gk. *zōē aiōnios*)is the positive eschatological destiny corresponding to an affirmative response to Jesus (sometimes shortened simply to "life"). On the other hand, "judgment" is the negative destiny corresponding to a rejection of Jesus. Both of these outcomes are evi-dent in John 3:16; when a person believes, he or she has "eternal life;" the default apart from believing is to "perish" (Gk. *apollymi*). John uses several terms corresponding to "perish." Persons may "be judged" (Gk. *krinō*), enter into "judgment" (Gk. *krisis*) or "die (Gk. *apothnēskō*) in their sins."

It might be a bit confusing that I put "eternal life" in the Destiny theme rather than the Life theme. The distinction comes based on whom that life is associated. If "life" is indicated as a characteristic of Jesus as giver of life, then we are dealing with the Life theme. If "life" becomes the outcome or destiny of a positive response to Jesus, then we are looking at the Destiny theme. Once again, the words themselves do not determine the theme to which they belong, but the context.

Another question that may arise concerns God's absolute love with regard to judgment. How does judgment cohere with God's absolute love for the world? Are they not polar opposites? Not for John. One must think about this issue in terms of experiencing God's love in two ways. God's love is absolute, but the way a person perceives and experi-ences God's love depends on one's viewpoint. I have often used a coin as an illustration. The way one describes a coin depends on which side of the coin one is observing. The "heads" side looks entirely different than the "tails" side. The coin is the same however and does not change. Your perspective determines how you experience that coin. How you experience God's love depends on how you have responded to that love, either with a believing or an unbelieving response. God's love does not change; love is inherent in God's character. How we perceive God's love is the issue. This consideration leads to a seeming paradox. God's love *encompasses* judgment. The person who experiences judgment is still within the realm of God's love, not outside of it. God's desire however is for the salvation of the world. God wants for all to experience God's love as life and not judgment.

An understanding of this important concept leads to a greater understanding of how Jesus interacted with people. The way Jesus communicated with people was based on what they needed. If they needed affirmation, he gave affirmation (Nathaniel in John 1 for example); if they needed gentle prods to open their minds, he did that, as in the instances of Nicodemus and the Samaritan woman. With the royal official of John 4 and the crowd in John 6, Jesus made provocative statements meant to bring out faith (4:48 and 6:26). In general, Jesus is fairly neutral but quite direct when speaking to the "crowd," as instanced in John 6:26–58, and even to the Jewish leaders, as in 8:12–29. The most problematic of Jesus' interactions are the highly confrontational and even polemical conversations with the Jewish leaders and in part with the "crowd" in Jerusalem. The prime examples appear in 5:41–47 and 8:30–59. Jesus' confrontational words, however, are the words the leaders need to hear. When Jesus tells the Jewish leaders they are "from your father the devil" (8:44), he is speaking of their current identity and trying to get them to change their identity (and destiny) by believing in him. He asks them pointedly a few verses later, "If I am speaking the truth, why don't you believe in me?" (8:46). Jesus is not confronting the Jews to condemn them but to shake them up and hopefully engender some sort of positive response. For John, every word of Jesus was a loving word meant to bring about knowledge of God and a believing response, so that the recipient's experience of God's love would be life rather than judgment.

THE FUTURE IS NOW AND NOW IS THE FUTURE

When we are considering the destinies of eternal life and judgment, we must remember that John thinks about them not as simply a far away future, but as a current reality. This intertwining of present and future is the heart of John's "continuous" eschatology. For John "now" determines the "future" and the "future" impinges on the "now." When a person places their faith in Jesus (by believing, following, seeing, knowing etc.), they "have eternal life." On the other hand, not believing means the person will perish.

If one is thinking in purely time-based terms, the phrase "eternal life" may elicit the idea of "to live forever." In one respect this viewpoint is correct, but only partially. Jesus speaks numerous times in John of being raised to life "at the last day" (6:39, 40, 44, 51; 11:24). This phrase, "at the last day," is the key phrase for the future in John (and corresponds to the Jewish theological concept of the resurrection from the dead). This future sense of "eternal life" appears throughout John. In John 4, Jesus tells the Samaritan woman that the one who drinks his water will never thirst "forever" (Gk. *eis ton aiōna*) and the crowd in John 6 that if they eat the bread from heaven they will "live forever." The phrase for "forever" occurs in this sense seven times in John (4:14; 6:51, 58; 8:51, 52; 10:28; 11:26), often with the Greek construction for "never" (Gk. *ou mē*) which makes the future assertion even more definitive. Jesus reinforces the future of "life" to the disciples when he tells them he is going to prepare a place for them in his Father's house (14:2–3).

John also makes the future judgment clear. There is a definite and explicit expectation of future judgment in John. In John 5, after speaking of the prerogatives of giving life and judging that the Father has given over to him, Jesus warns the Jewish leaders, "An hour is coming when all those in the tombs will hear [the Son of Man's] voice, and those doing good will come out to a resurrection of life and those doing evil to a resurrection of judgment" (5:28–29). In the dispute with the Jewish leaders in John 8, Jesus speaks of going where they cannot come. They will "die in their sins" if they do not believe (8:21, 24). John emphasizes this future judgment by placing it in Jesus' closing words to the world in John 12:44–51: "the one who rejects me and does not receive my words has something that judges him; the word which I speak, that will judge him at the last day."

While John never lets the reader forget the future, he is even more concerned with the quality of eternal life as a present lived reality. Eternal life is not only a line extending to the future, but a life lived at this moment as God's life in you in all its fullness. Whatever the future holds can be lived now and indeed, the decision you make now is the key to your future (3:18). Eternal life now is the important result of being "born of God" (1:13) or "born from above/again" (3:2, 7). One's life and identity in the here and now is substantively changed from judgment to one of "abundant life" (10:10) or "a spring of water welling up to eternal life" (4:14). The very language of believing, seeing, knowing, following and remaining is present tense language meant to evoke the sense of an ongoing present reality. The imagery in John 15 may demonstrate this present reality in the most expressive way. Jesus is preparing his disciples for his departure and speaks of himself as a vine through whom on-going life flows to the disciples. "I am the vine, you are the branches," he tells them; "the one remaining in me and I in him, this one bears much fruit" (15:5). Throughout, the use of the verb "remain" (Gk. *menō*) indicates a deep, connected and life-giving relationship between Jesus and the disciples that results in "fruit" expressed by love for one another.

In contrast, judgment is not just an event that will happen in the future, but itself is a current state. John 3:18 contains a short three letter adverb, Gk. *ēdē*, that we translate as "already" or "now": "the one who believes in him is not judged, but the one who does not believe is *already* judged, because he has not believed in the only Son of God." For John, the natural state of the world is judgment. When God through Christ judges at the last day, any negative judgment will not be new, but simply an affirmation of what existed before. In this gospel, there is not what could be called an active judgment. The final verse of John 3 reiterates this observation: "The one believing the Son has life, but the one not believing the Son will not see life, but the wrath of God *remains* upon him." The "wrath" of God is a current reality for the person who has not made a positive response. Judgment is the default setting. The language of "you will die in your sins" in 8:21, 24, somewhat bridges the gap between the now and the future. Those who do not believe exist currently in a state of sin and in the future will die in that same state, with the reality of the "last day" ahead. John makes it clear that God's desire is for that state of sin and judgment to change in the present so that eternal life will become a reality in the present and in every moment into the forever.

PREDESTINY?

In some respects, all sounds well and good theologically. If a person chooses life, that person gets life; if judgment, judgment. But who *chooses* life? The world seems bent on judgment. The Prologue indicates that the world did not know the *Logos* and his own people did not accept him. Later we read that, "people loved the darkness rather than the light." So who *chooses* life? John has an answer, albeit a very difficult one for many: those who believe, believe because God chose them and "birthed" them. Now those from a Reformed perspective will readily affirm this position; of course God chooses who will believe! But there is a real problem for that perspective also in the Destiny theme. God's desire is for the world to be saved, not judged (3:17). The Destiny theme includes all of the material related to the issue of so-called predestination (though the term does not occur in John) and one must carefully consider all of the evidence before coming to any conclusions.

One of the conundrums that John wrestles with throughout is unbelief. If Jesus is "the Way, the Truth, and the Life," why do most people not perceive who he is and put their faith in him; on the other hand why the positive response from those who do believe? At various places in the gospel, John explores this issue either through the words of Jesus or in his own commentary. Although John does not explicitly deal with this question before chapter three, he lays the foundation for it. We already see the tension in the Prologue between those who do not know or receive the Logos (1:10–11) and "as many as received him . . . to those who believed in his name . . . who were born from God" (1:12–13). Later in John 1 we see the Baptist's disciples turn to follow Jesus, and then see Jesus calling disciples. In John 2, we see a believing response from the disciples, an implied rejection from the Jewish leaders, and even a "positive" response from the people, which Jesus does not trust. Then in the first part of John 3, we read of the inquirer Nicodemus who cannot seem to understand what Jesus is talking about with regard to being "born again" and "born of water and Spirit." Indeed, there appears to be a major gulf between Jesus and Nicodemus, the gulf of heavenly and earthly understanding. John never tells us if Nicodemus "got it," though he may imply this reality later in the gospel.

John 3:16 also implies this tension, but does not solve it. When we read, "so that all who believe might not perish, but have eternal life," is the "all" referring to everyone, or to those God has specifically chosen and called to believe in distinction to the rest of humanity who are not? The emphasis appears to be on choice in 3:18; John places an equal emphasis on the one who believes and the one who does not. In 3:19–21, however, John reasons why most do not choose and why some do. Most do not because they "loved the darkness" and they hate the light and do not approach the light because of their evil deeds. For those who practice the good, however, it is because *their works were brought about by God* (3:21). Here we have the first clear indication of God's hand in the action of believing, which is in fact the content of "works" (see 6:29). John gives us one other small notice for this part of the Destiny theme in 3:35–36. There we read that, "the Father loves the Son and has given all things into his hands. The one believing in the Son has eternal life, but the one not believing will not see life." There appears to be a connection, albeit unclear, between the "giving all things into his hands" and those who believe (and perhaps those who do not).

During Jesus defense of himself before the Jewish leaders in John 5, though we clearly see that the Father "has given all judgment to the Son" (5:22), the overwhelming emphasis in this section appears to be on the will to believe on the part of the listeners. Indeed, what Jesus speaks to the Jewish leaders is spoken "so you might be saved" (5:34)! Their lack of belief comes as a result of their own unwillingness to consider Jesus' claims, despite Jesus' assertion that Moses affirmed those very claims.

John 6 is where this aspect of the Destiny theme is most acutely present. After proclaiming himself to be "the Bread of Life" and the invitation that "the one who comes to me will never hunger and the one who believes in me will never thirst" (6:35), Jesus makes the observation that "you have seen me and have not believed" (6:36). Why? He adds, "Everyone whom the Father gives to me comes to me" (6:37). We have what appears to be a clear statement of divine destiny for those who believe. Jesus goes on to affirm that, "this is the will of the one who sent me, that everyone he has given me I will not lose from him, but will raise [them] at the last day" (6:39). When his Jewish listeners begin to "grumble," Jesus makes the point even sharper, "no one is able to come to me except that the Father who sent me draws him, and I will raise him at the last day" (6:44). With the mention of "the last day" in these examples, we are obviously concerned with the Destiny theme. Now the notion of a person freely choosing their destiny appears to be a chimera.

A person does not believe unless he or she is "given" and "drawn" by the Father.

Is John setting out an absolute determinism here, at least in terms of who will believe? Taken alone perhaps yes, but even immediately following 6:44, Jesus sets out a balancing statement, "everyone will be taught by God; everyone who hears from my Father and learns, comes to me" (6:45). Further, we see that the Father's "drawing" comes via the cross, where Jesus says, "I will draw all men to myself" (12:32). In the concluding words of John 6, Jesus tells his disciples, "have I not chosen you twelve (yet one of you is a devil)." Though Jesus' words may refer to his choice of these particular disciples, the sentiment is consistent with the rest of the chapter where both sides of choosing and choice evident. Later, we discover that Judas's choice to betray Jesus is consistent with scriptural warrant. But Judas made the choice himself.

John 10 only adds to this supposition of God's participation and direction in the process of believing. Jesus knows his "sheep" and his sheep know him (10:14); he lays down his life for them (15) and they hear his voice and follow him (27). None of the sheep will ever perish for no one can take away what the Father has given (29). Later in John 15, Jesus tells his disciples, "You have not chosen me, but I have chosen you and appointed you to go and bear fruit" (15:16). Finally, in John 17, Jesus refers to all God has given to him, so he might give eternal life to them (17:2). Indeed his prayer is not for the world, but "for those you have given me" (17:9; also 11, 12, 24). The balance to these set-apart believers however is the mission purpose of their being sent into the world (17:18) so that "the world might believe that you sent me" (17:20).

John brings one more comment to this issue in 12:37–43 that adds greater weight to the idea of predestination. John seeks to give a reason for those who do not believe. As in the Synoptic Gospels (Matt 13:14–15, Mark 4:12, Luke 8:8), Acts (28:26–27), and Paul (Rom 10:16; 11:8), John draws on the prophet Isaiah to explain unbelief. John argues that the lack of response was in line what Isaiah had prophesied in Isa 53:1 and Isa 6:10, thus "they were unable to believe" (12:39) despite the signs Jesus had done in their presence (12:37). This unbelief occurs because, "he has blinded their eyes and hardened their hearts, lest they see with their eyes and perceive with their hearts . . ." Indeed, in John's view, Isaiah spoke these words specifically regarding Jesus (12:41) and "his glory," a likely reference to Isaiah's encounter with the glory of God in Isa 6. Further, this lack of belief fits within God's purposes; unbelief had to happen. Though John does not out and out say it, the hour/glorification/lifting up of the Son of Man came about as the result of willful rejection of Jesus, a rejection that was fully in the plan of God.

Taken alone, one might posit a stark double predestination here. That would be wrong, however. The context of the passage leaves significant ambiguity for this proposition. First, the "they" of 12:37 and 39 is undefined with regard to specific individuals. John speaks of the Jewish people as representative of the world as a whole here, not as individuals. Indeed, surrounding this passage, John refers to those who do believe. More significant is the continued plea of Jesus on both sides of this section for his listeners to respond to his message: "believe in the light, so you might become sons of light" (12:36); "I am the light of the world, so that everyone who believes in me might not remain in darkness" (12:46). To the very end of his ministry and in his commission to his followers, Jesus never gives up on the world.

What can one conclude from this evidence? John has a definite sense that the destiny of those who have believed is not a simple act of choosing to believe but includes the active hand of God. But neither does the responsibility for believing totally belong to God. The emphasis on believing throughout the gospel and Jesus' constant insistence on believing puts our active choice as part of the salvation process. Likewise for John, unbelief simply cannot be attributed to predestination. The world's retreat from the truth and its love for the darkness are reasons enough.

CONCLUSION

The Destiny theme is a difficult theme, both in terms of the imagery/ motifs involved and in the clarity of its meaning. The theme fundamentally concerns eschatology, or more specifically the destiny of the world to either life or judgment. God's desire, based on his absolute love for the world, is that the world should have life. To that end, he sent his Son to fulfill a specific destiny, the cross, and by fulfilling it to open the way to "life" for the world. This life is not just a future hope, but begins in the present, at the moment when the one who believes is "born of God." Abundant life is the present result that continues beyond physical death to a resurrection of life "at the last day." The experience of God's love as life, however, is predicated on a positive response to the Son, Jesus. Otherwise, the experience is that of remaining in judgment and to a "resurrection of judgment." Those who do believe cannot claim this salvation on the merits of belief because God the Father is fully active in drawing and giving those who believe to the Son, who will never let them go. On the other side, though a response of rejection fits clearly within the purposes of God, the actual rejection comes not because God does not invite and even draw, but because people "loved the darkness rather than the light." Despite rejection, God continues to invite the world to experience his love as life.

PART TWO

Studies

THE FOLLOWING STUDIES EXAMINE selected sections of John with regard to how John interweaves the themes together to create his complex theology. My hope is that these studies will model how to study all of John using the themes as a guide. Once again, I encourage you to mark your copy of John with different colors and comments as you identify the different themes in the text in interaction with each other and in support of John's purpose in writing the gospel.

8

A Thematic Analysis of John 3:1–21

CHAPTER 3 OF THE Gospel of John stands as one of the most theologically dense sections of the gospel and, one might argue, of the writings of the New Testament, comparable to Romans 3 or 8. John conveys this theological density, however, within a narrative format infused with every theme we have discussed in Part One. John 3 contains no sign or action of Jesus, just a great deal of speech. Nevertheless, this chapter of John may be the most well known because of the inclusion of 3:16, arguably the most quoted verse in the Bible. The importance of 3:16 is no mistake; it serves as a kind of fulcrum for this chapter and as an adequate summary for the message of the entire gospel, comparable to 20:31, but much more theologically direct. This section of John picks up themes such as Life and Destiny that were introduced in the Prologue but not expanded in any detail in the sections on the calling of the disciples, the water to wine miracle and the temple cleansing episode. The most remarkable feature of this chapter is its weaving together of all the themes in a distinctly "Johannine" way that we do not see again until the conclusion of the "Book of Signs" in 12:44–50. Also notable are patterns of speech that become the norm for Jesus' speech in the remainder of John, especially language related to themes of Life, Believing, and Destiny.

Two major sections comprise John 3. The first section begins with a conversation between Jesus and the Pharisee Nicodemus and then concludes with the theological implications of that conversation; the second section relates an incident involving John the Baptist and its theological implications. In this study we will consider the first section.

John 3 is actually a continuation of 2:23–24. The standard Greek text shows no paragraph break between 2:25 and 3:1. In those three verses John has woven the Festival, Believing, Signs and Witness themes together in a way that expressed a putative positive response to Jesus' signs, but with a question of whether the response was truly authentic: "Jesus did not entrust himself to them . . . for he knew what was in a man." Without a break chapter 3 begins immediately with the words, "There was a man . . ." The conversation with Nicodemus illustrates why Jesus did not entrust himself to them.

NICODEMUS

When John introduces Nicodemus as "a man from the Pharisees . . . a ruler of the Jews," he is invoking the Festival theme. Nicodemus is representative of the Jewish leadership. Indeed, Nicodemus speaks with the plural "we," suggesting he is a conscious representative of that group. The conversation from 3:1–13 shows the disparity between the understanding of the Jewish leadership and Jesus. In 3:10 Jesus asks, "Are you the teacher of Israel and you do not know these things?" The implication John conveys is that Jesus is the replacement for the Jewish leadership. Later in John 10 this implication is made complete when Jesus identifies himself as "the good shepherd" and the Jewish leadership as hired hands, thieves and murderers.

In verse 2, the narrator makes the comment that "[Nicodemus] came to [Jesus] at *night*." Some would see this phrase as part of the motif of light/darkness by which John makes a subtle statement on the condition of Nicodemus' spiritual state. Nevertheless, Nicodemus makes the seemingly perceptive statement: "Rabbi, we know that you are a teacher come from God." Nicodemus acknowledges Jesus' status as a respected Jewish teacher, but more importantly one "from God." Two themes are evident here. "We *know*" is from the Believing theme and "a teacher come from God" is a statement of Identity. It is not clear whether Nicodemus speaks from true knowledge or not. Is this statement intended to "butter" Jesus up, or do the Pharisees represented by Nicodemus actually believe Jesus is from God?

The basis of Nicodemus' statement is identified in the next phrase, "for no one can perform these signs . . . except that God is with him." John invokes the Signs theme whereby there is some sort of response to the signs, but a question as to whether that response is authentic (see above comment on 2:23–25). The ensuing conversation with Jesus suggests at best misunderstanding, and at worst no belief at all, though later in the gospel, Nicodemus does at least appear to be a sincere inquirer (see John 7:50; 19:39).

In 3:3, Jesus actually fulfills Nicodemus' positive assessment by abruptly changing from Nicodemus' mention of his signs to true teaching from God: "Truly, truly I tell you, no one can see the kingdom of God without being born from above." Jesus introduces his statement with the Witness theme phrase "Truly, truly I say to you" (Gk. *amēn, amēn legō hymin*), a phrase that often introduces a key traditional statement of Jesus (cf. Mt 18:3), and in every case is one to be taken as very important. An interesting aspect of Jesus' response is that he repeats features of Nicodemus' statement, though in reverse order: "Unless God is with him" becomes "unless a person is born from above." "No one is able to do these things" becomes, "No one can see the kingdom of God." Jesus has moved the conversation from a focus on Signs to a focus on Life from God. Nicodemus is coming to conclusions about Jesus from observation of earthly things, whereas Jesus wants Nicodemus to understand where true life from God comes from.

Identity is still at issue here because of a likely *double entendre*. The first element of the double meaning comes in that Jesus himself is the only-begotten of God and already sees the Kingdom of God (see 3:13). The second meaning relates to those who have "received him" and thus become children of God, because they are born from God (1:12–13). "Born from above" (Gk. *gennēthē anōthen*, often translated "born again") shows a use of the Identity theme related to the believer in Jesus: the identity of a person "born from above" has changed from an earthly origin to a heavenly one (cf. "born from God" in 1:13).

"The Kingdom of God" is an image related to the Life and Destiny themes. The phrase, a very common one in the Synoptic Gospels and the topic of many parables there, is never extended into a motif in the Gospel of John until the passion narrative in Jesus' conversation with Pilate ("My kingdom is not of this world") and later the placard upon the cross where Jesus is proclaimed "King of the Jews." The more common phrase "eternal life," introduced in 3:15, is for John the expression that most closely parallels "the Kingdom of God."

"See" (Gk. *oraō*) is part of the Believing theme. Though Jesus replaces "see" with "enter" in 3:5, here in 3:3, "see" must be looked at in its own right, as God-given sight to perceive what his kingdom is. This "seeing" is not natural sight but the sight that comes from spiritual birth.

With this statement from Jesus in 3:3, John is subtly preparing for the introduction of the Destiny theme in 3:16–21. To be born from above is God's action, not a human one, as the conversation with Nicodemus continues to imply. What then is the relationship between God's action and man's action?

Nicodemus' response is partially indicative of the answer to that question. The NRSV rightly translates the Greek *anothen* as "from above." The term can also mean "again" (as in most translations) and indeed, Nicodemus takes Jesus' statement as "born again" because he does not conceive of the other sense. In asking "How is a man able to be born when he is old?" Nicodemus is unable to bridge the conceptual gap that Jesus presents in his statement. Nicodemus becomes one of a number of characters in the gospel to exhibit a misunderstanding (e.g., the Jewish leaders in 1:20; the Samaritan woman in 4:15). He does not know what Jesus is speaking about.

Jesus pointedly intensifies this conceptual gap in his succeeding statements. In 3:5 Jesus essentially repeats verse 3, but replaces "born from above" with "born from water and spirit" and replaces "see" with "enter" (Gk. *eiserchomai*). The replacement words are consistent with the themes of Life (water, Spirit) and Believing (enter). Water and spirit are oblique terms at this point in John, but later in 4:10–26 and 7:39–39, water and Spirit are closely allied with the person of Jesus as the giver of life. In the starkly dualistic statement that follows in 3:6 Jesus contrasts physical life ("born of the flesh") with Spirit-given life ("born of the Spirit"), and presses the point in 3:8 that this spiritual birth only comes from the ineffable work of the Spirit. The source of true Life is God alone.

John 3:8 continues to develop the *double entendre* of 3:3 and adds a second one. In a parable-like comparison, Jesus compares the Spirit to the wind—an actual play on words in Greek since *pneuma* means either wind or spirit. Neither the physical wind nor the Spirit can be pinned down in terms of source or destination. The same applies to those "born of the Spirit." Once again the language here can refer either to Jesus or the believer in Jesus ("*everyone* who is born of the Spirit"). The phrase "where it comes from or where it goes" is typical language of the Identity theme in John. In 8:14 the language is remarkably similar: "Jesus answered, 'Even if I testify on my own behalf, my testimony is valid because I know where I have come from and where I am going, but you do not know where I come from or where I am going.'" Jesus comes from the Father and will return to the Father. Likewise, those born of the Spirit now have an origin and a destiny in God.

The misunderstanding by Nicodemus continues in 3:9 ("how can these things be") and Jesus responds by joining the Festival and Believing themes. He asks, "are you a teacher of Israel and you do not understand these things?" (3:10). Of all people, the Pharisees as devoted students of the Jewish scriptures should be aware of the movement of the Spirit. Instead there is a wide gulf between their understanding and true spiritual reality. The depth of this gulf is apparent in 3:11–12, drawing on language of the Witness and Believing themes. Jesus once again introduces with the Witness phrase "Truly, truly, I tell you," and then continues the theme with "we speak of what we know and testify to what we have seen; yet you do not receive our testimony." Jesus' words use the exclusive plural "we" and the plural form of "you." Scholars are divided over the reason for and the makeup of the "we." Does it refer to Jesus, the Father, and the Spirit? Does it refer to Jesus and his followers? Reference to 5:31–47 might indicate some of both: there the testimony to Jesus includes the witness of John and the Father (as well as Jesus' signs and the Jewish scriptures).[1] The content of Jesus' witness comes from knowing and seeing spiritual realities, but those Nicodemus represents do not receive the witness. The interplay of the Witness and Believing themes was first set out in the Prologue in 1:5–12. Here in the Nicodemus story we can detect the continuing rejection of the witness indicated in 1:11, "he came to his own place, and his own people did not accept him" (cf. 2:18–20). This rejection will continue throughout the gospel.

Jesus reiterates the dualistic gulf between himself and Nicodemus in verse 12, continuing the Witness-Believing theme interaction ("tell" and "believe). "Earthly things" are likely the symbolic or parable-like comparisons that Jesus has been trying to convey to Nicodemus (i.e. birth/born from above and wind/Spirit). Without a basic understanding and reception of this information, deeper spiritual teaching is useless.

Despite his statement in 3:12, Jesus proceeds to make the pronouncement of a heavenly reality in 3:13: "Indeed, no one has ascended

---

1. Several respected scholars, such as J. L. Martyn, R. Brown and C. K. Barrett, argue for a "two-level" historical referent here with Jesus and Nicodemus in view on the one hand, and Jesus followers in interaction with the later synagogue Jews many years later on the other. This reading seems overly speculative, so I am inclined to see an inner-textual referent as indicated.

into heaven, except the one who has descended from heaven, the Son of Man." This pronouncement is that of Identity; it may be one of the most important Identity statements in the gospel. Jesus' words invoke the "descent and ascent of the Son of Man" motif. This motif is first present in 1:51 where the angels ascend and descend upon the Son of Man, suggesting that this "Son of Man" is the embodiment of Jacob's ladder as the way to heaven. Here the picture is a bit different. In speaking to Nicodemus, Jesus is giving the basis for his understanding of "heavenly things." He as the Son of Man is the only being ever descended *from* heaven (cf. 1:14). His ascension to heaven is implied to be subsequent to his descent from heaven, where the Son of Man existed from the beginning as the *Logos* (1:1).

To the first century Jewish reader, the Festival theme may be in view. A number of works known as apocalypses (Daniel and Revelation are canonical examples) often contained heavenly journeys, where the purported writer of the apocalypse is taken to heaven, shown various heavenly scenes, then returns to report on the journey. Recent scholarship has also concluded that a growing interest in mystical visions and journeys based on the throne imagery from Ezekiel 1 existed among some Jewish groups. John seems to be implying with this statement of Jesus that Jesus' knowledge of heavenly realities trumps and replaces any claims of knowledge based on mystical visionary ascents, because he is the one from heaven.[2]

The next two verses (3:14–15) form the likely conclusion to Jesus' conversation with Nicodemus (see below). These verses make up one three-clause sentence which brings together five themes (Identity, Life, Festival, Believing, Destiny) to form a dense theological statement encompassing Revelation and Response. In 3:14, the Festival theme comes clearly into view along with Identity. The figure of the Son of Man, descended from heaven in 3:13, is now set in a typological comparison with an Old Testament image, the bronze serpent lifted up on a pole in Numbers 28:8–9 which brought healing to those Israelites who gazed upon it ("whenever a serpent bit someone, that person would look at the serpent of bronze and live"). The comparison is made with the conjunctions, "just as...so" as well as with the repeated verb "to lift up" (Gk. *hypsoō*). In similar fashion to the OT event, now the Son of Man must be lifted up. This statement is the first of three occasions where Jesus refers

2. See Rowland, "The Mystical Element," 123–31.

to the necessity for the Son of Man to be lifted up (see 8:28 and 12:32, 34—in 12:32, "I" is present instead of "the Son of Man"). This "lifting up" is a Life theme image making reference to the crucifixion and reminiscent of the servant passage in Isaiah 52:13–15.

Verse 15 ties the typological comparison of 14 together: "so that everyone who believes in him might have eternal life." As the Israelites looked at the serpent and lived, now those who believe in the Son of Man will gain eternal life. The themes of Believing and Destiny join the mix. Jesus speaks of the Destiny phrase "eternal life," a phrase used a dozen times in John that usually occurs along with a verb from the Believing theme. These two verses thus connect Jesus' identity as the Son of Man with an OT image (the bronze snake), both of which are lifted up and bring life to those who believe. This Festival theme image is the third one that ultimately connects to the crucifixion. Previously John the Baptist makes reference to "the Lamb of God" and then Jesus makes the statement "destroy this temple and in three days I will raise it."

GOD SO LOVED THE WORLD . . .

Taken together 3:14–15 summarizes the gospel message. A restatement of this message comes in 3:16 and in various ways throughout the gospel (see Appendix: The Gospel Summaries in John). In all of the gospel summary statements John includes at least the Identity, Believing and Destiny themes and usually one other theme.

John 3:16, perhaps the most recognizable verse in the Bible, is an important summary of the gospel as just indicated. But one must not read the verse in isolation—these words continue the thought of 3:14–15 and at the same time introduce one of the most important theological passages in John and arguably the NT. John 3:16–21 contains a rich mix of themes including the essential introduction of the Destiny theme.

As the conversation with Nicodemus unfolds it is difficult to tell where the conversation ends and the gospel writer begins commentary. Most scholars see a break between 3:15 and 3:16, while others (and most red letter bibles) continue the words of Jesus until 3:21. Grammatically there is no break, though there are several other clues that may suggest a break including a slight thematic shift. For the first time in the gospel, "God" is the subject of a sentence. In addition, it is the first time "love" is used and the first time since chapter 1 that "world" is used. Further, the writer has not used "only-begotten" since the Prologue in 1:14 and 18.

Taken together, it appears that John is moving from a statement of Jesus in 3:14–15 and rephrasing the content to deepen the thematic mix using distinct vocabulary that clarifies the gospel message just summarized in 3:14–15.

The "for" (Gk. *gar*) at the beginning of 3:16 is a conjunction used to connect this verse with 3:14–15 and explain them further. There is also something of a loosely parallel structure to 3:14–15, in that there are three clauses. But in the first phrase of 3:16, instead of Moses as the actor, God is the main actor. While Moses showed concern for the people of Israel, God "loved the world". Here we have the Festival theme writ large and breaking the bounds of the Old Testament. God's steadfast love for Israel is now proclaimed as a universal love for all humanity.

The phrase "For God so loved the world" is as importantly the introduction of the Destiny theme. In the explanation of the Destiny theme I posited that the love of God for humanity is not something that is ever absent—it simply is, it is absolute, for as 1 John says, "God is love." The question is not "Does God love me?" but rather, "how do I receive the love of God?" Or, using the language of the theme, "based on God's love and my response, what is my destiny?" The end of 3:16 provides a hint, but it is the following verses of 3:17–21 where John explores this latter question.

As noted above, the verb "love" (Gk. *agapaō*) appears for the first time in 3:16. This use is the only instance in the gospel where the object of God's love is "the world." Thereafter, John utilizes "love" to describe the relationship of the Father for the Son and vice versa, and later of Jesus' (and the Father's) love for the disciples or the disciples' love for Jesus. The theme that "love" goes with varies, depending of the subject and object. When the relationship is the Father and Son, the Identity theme is indicated. Where Jesus loves the disciples, the Life theme is evident and in the case of the disciples' love for Jesus (and the Father), we see the Believing theme. Here in 3:16 both the Life and Destiny themes are in view. "Love" is a life-inducing characteristic of God that offers the destiny of eternal life.

Notice that I have been using the term "humanity" interchangeably with "world." While "world" (Gk. *kosmos*) has a number of different denotations, even in John, here the term is similar to its use in 1:9–10 and phrases such as "Behold, the Lamb of God, who takes away the sin of the world," "the Savior of the world," and "the Light of the world." In each case, the referent is primarily, if not exclusively, the world of humanity. The close proximity of "world" and "people" (Gk. *anthrōpoi*) in 3:19 makes this identification clear. The world of humanity is generally either a neutral or negative concept in John. Tending toward the negative are places like 1:9–10 where the world does not know the *Logos*, or later, when Jesus tells the disciples that the world will hate them because they hated him (15:18). Despite this negative connotation, God does not view the world negatively from the perspective of his love. Not only is this perspective evident here in 3:16 but also in the phrases just mentioned such as Lamb of God, Savior, and Light, as well as other images (e.g. 6:33). The world may reject and hate God, but this rejection never negates the actual love of God.

The next phrase in 3:16 is the explanation of how God "so" (Gk. *houtōs*) loved the world, or better, how God loved the world "in this way." "That he gave his only Son" is the way God loved the world. The phrase is loosely parallel to "so it is necessary for the Son of Man to be lifted up" in 3:14. In both phrases it is the Son who receives the action and in both cases God is the instigator of the action (though in 3:14 God is an implied agent). The phrase is also partially paralleled in the succeeding verse with the phrase, "God did not send the Son into the world to condemn the world . . . " The three verbs, "lifted up," "gave," and "send," are all actions of God with the Son as the object. But the three verbs have slightly different senses and relate to different themes. I have already pointed out that "lifted up" relates to the Festival theme and, in the purpose of this action on the cross, to the Life theme. "Gave" in 3:16 is a term full of meaning. On the one hand, it is quite similar to "lifted up" in the respect that the Life theme is in view based on the purpose of bringing "eternal life." God gave Jesus on the cross to bring salvation to humanity. But "gave" also relates to the Identity theme since the origin of the Son is clearly set out here: "that he gave his *only-begotten* Son." Translations are varied in the rendering of the Greek *monogenēs* (only, one and only, only-begotten), but the idea is that the Son is unique with relation to God as opposed to the more generic sense meaning "a child of God." This phrase is related to the incarnational statement in 1:14: "And the Word became flesh and dwelled among us, full of grace and truth; and we beheld his glory, glory as of the only-begotten from the Father." This particular connection is reflected in the repetition of "only-begotten" in 1:14 and 18, and 3:16 and 18. The purpose of the incarnation was to make God known (1:18). Thus when God "gave his only-begotten Son," he revealed himself as God who loves the world in the *Logos* made flesh; he exemplified this love by giving his Son on the cross for the salvation of the world.

The third clause in 3:16 shows the ultimate purpose for which God gave his only Son and is parallel to the purpose clause in 3:15, "that everyone who believes in him may have eternal life." The words in 3:16 are in fact a virtual repetition, "that everyone who believes in him . . . may have eternal life."[3] Thus we have in this clause a reiteration of the Believing and Destiny themes. Just as a reminder, "eternal life" belongs to the Destiny theme rather the Life theme since it is an outcome. The Life theme refers to the characteristics inherent in Jesus as the life-giving Savior.

In 3:16, this purpose clause is actually more intricate than 3:15 in that it is composed of two parts joined by the conjunction "but" (Gk. *alla*). John inserts an additional phrase that is opposite of "may have eternal life." The words "may not perish" produce another layer of complexity that brings into question what the love of God entails. We are faced with the Destiny theme in its full reality here. God's love in giving his Son is intended to bring life, but the possibility of destruction is always in view. The implication here is that eternal life is conditioned upon believing in the only Son. The default setting is being destroyed (or "perishing" Gk. *apollymi*). Does the possibility of destruction negate God's love? Is God's love therefore absent or ineffective in the case of those who do not believe? The following verses delve into these questions to an extent, but do not fully answer them. As an interim assessment I will simply note again that God's love for the world stands absolutely, despite the world's response to God's action whether believing or not believing. It is not the presence or absence of God's love at issue, but the way God's love manifests itself eschatologically with respect to the world of humanity and its responses.

As 3:16 restated in a universal fashion what Jesus said in 3:14–15, now 3:17 reiterates 3:16 using the slightly different thematic emphasis of the Witness and Destiny themes. The "lifted up" of 3:14 and the "gave" of 3:16 now becomes "send," part of the Witness theme. Before this point in the gospel, the only one God had "sent" was John the Baptist (1:5; 33; 3:28). Now we have the first of 20 instances where God (usually "the

---

3. The only difference is noticeable in Greek where 3:15 has *en autō* "in him" and 3:16 has *eis auton* "in(to) him." The phrases are synonymous in meaning.

Father") sends his Son. God has sent his Son on a mission to witness to God and his saving purposes.

As in 3:16 (and 3:14–15), the action of God vis-à-vis the Son is followed by the purpose of the action ("so that," "to" or "in order that"; Gk. *hina*). The composition of 3:17 is somewhat strange, however, because of the negative: "For God did *not* send his Son into the world to condemn the world, but in order that the world might be saved through him." In using the negation, John sets up a "not this, but that" contrast which places emphasis on the positive purpose of God's love. The loving action of God is intended to bring salvation and life. At the same time John is once again implying the reality of judgment and the "dark side" of the Destiny theme.

John has now stated gospel summaries in three parallel sentences. The "good news" is that God has acted in his Son to bring healing, life, and salvation to those who respond in belief. The "bad news" is the default judgment apart from believing. This default condemnation is not God's purpose, but is nevertheless real and ultimately must be incorporated into an understanding of God's love.

AND THIS IS THE JUDGMENT

The final four verses of this section excavate more deeply into the Destiny theme by more pointedly stressing the reality of judgment and attempting to explain why much of humanity does not respond to God's loving action. The Destiny theme is set in tandem with other themes and in doing so different facets of the Destiny theme become evident.

In 3:18 John places the Destiny and Believing themes together in both positive and negative formulations. "Those who believe in him are not condemned," reiterates the saving purpose of God and the response of believing that brings God's purpose to fruition. But here "not condemned" is used instead of "saved." This statement sets up the primary declaration in the verse, which focuses on judgment: "But those who do not believe are condemned already, because they have not believed in the name of the only Son of God." Here John clearly declares the default setting of judgment with the word "already." Notice that John has changed to the passive voice in this verse. Whereas God is clearly the subject of the action in 3:14–17, here God is not necessarily the subject of "condemned." God does not actively condemn, but allows for an already-in-place condemnation as a result of a negative response to God's loving action in the sending of his only Son.

The last three verses (3:19–21) place the Destiny and Life themes together, primarily using the dualistic contrast of light and darkness. Instead of the verb "condemn" (Gk. *krinō*), John uses the related noun "judgment" (Gk. *krisis*). This "judgment" is a statement of the facts with regard to the light and the response to the light: "the light has come into the world and people loved the darkness rather than the light, for their deeds were evil." "Light" alludes back to the prologue (1:4, 5, and esp. 9 "he was the true light coming into the world") and forward to Jesus' pronouncement, "I am the Light of the world" in 8:12 and 9:4. God gave, sent, and lifted up his only Son, the Light that has come to the world. The Life theme shines brilliantly as this passage develops. God's love for the world never flags but continues to display itself. The contrast, however, is that darkness remains and humanity loved (Gk. *agapaō*!) the darkness instead of the light. Why? "For their deeds were evil." Here the uncomfortable ambiguity of the Destiny theme is evident: are people evil by choice or by destiny?

Continuing the thought of 3:18–19, verses 20 and 21 are essentially parallel in their structure but present a stark dualism with relation to the destiny of people. Verse 20 adds to the facts of 19: "For everyone who practices evil hates the light and does not come to the light, so that their works might not be exposed." "Hates" and "does not come" are negative statements of the Believing theme. The question that once again presents itself is whether "practicing evil" is by choice or destiny? In either case, people do not come for a reason: they do not want their evil deeds exposed.

Finally, 3:21 only confirms the ambiguity of the Destiny theme: "but the one doing the truth comes to the light, so that his works might be revealed that they were wrought by God." This punctuating verse to 3:1–21 is composed of a rich combination of the Witness, Believing, Life, and Destiny themes, with the emphasis on the Destiny theme. The nature of "the one doing the truth" (Witness theme) is imprecise with regard to time. Does the person come because he does the truth, does he do the truth by coming to the light, or does one do the truth as a consequence of coming to the light? The present tenses of the participle "the one who does" (from Gk. *poieo*) together with the verb "come" (Gk. *erchomai*) present any of these three possibilities. Those who do come to the light (Believing and Life themes) come in fulfillment of a divine purpose, "so that the person's works might be shown to have been done by God." God's own work is ultimately the source of those doing the truth and coming to the Light.

The Destiny theme is conspicuously evident here, but the ultimate conclusion of an absolute predestination cannot be held. John still never answers the question of choice or (pre)destiny. What one can say from this passage is that God loves the world, his purpose is for the world to be saved through his only Son, and that those who do ultimately come to the light do so because God has worked graciously in that person. What one *cannot* say from these verses is that God is not working graciously to bring about his purpose of salvation to all of humanity. John states the positive, but not the negative. The negative is only connected to those who do not respond: they are "already condemned" by their negative response. But even in this state of condemnation, John does not restrict the possibility of a future response, however improbable. In the rest of John, Jesus continues to communicate the love of God to the receptive and non-receptive. This passage goes to the heart of the so-called Calvinist-Armenian divide. The remainder of John occasionally adds further material for the Destiny theme but never ultimately decides for one side of the divide or the other.

This study of John 3:1–21 has illustrated how the gospel writer has developed his theological emphases through the interweaving of all seven themes discussed in the first section. Though every section of John does not have exhibit the density of themes that 3:1–21 does, every section does contain some of the themes and identifying them aids the student in understanding the theology of John in a deeper way.

9

A Thematic Analysis of John 6:26–58

JOHN 6 STANDS AT the center of the public ministry of Jesus in the scheme of John's chronology. Despite being the longest chapter in the gospel, John 6 is clearly a discreet literary unit that starts with a "sign," develops the symbolism of the sign and ends with the ultimate responses to the sign. In this analysis, I will focus on the interaction of themes in the middle portion of the chapter comprising 6:26–58, usually called the "Bread of Life" discourse.

The opening sign of John 6 is the feeding of the multitudes by the Sea of Galilee. I have interpreted John's account of this miracle as part of the Life theme, though there are also elements of Festival, Believing, Signs, and even Destiny themes in the telling. Literarily, John intends for this miraculous feeding to set the stage for a discussion about the identity of Jesus in 6:26–58 that revolves around the motif of bread.

A second miraculous event, Jesus' walking on the sea, takes place between the feeding miracle and the discussion. Scholars have debated John's intent in including this account. At the least, it serves two functions. One John uses the story to change settings from one side of the lake to the other. Since both the feeding story and this story take place in the context of Passover, there may be an allusion to the Exodus crossing of the Red Sea. Two, the story serves to distinguish the disciples from the crowd. In this story Jesus says to the disciples "I am, do not fear" (6:20), which may imply the divine name, rather than simply "It's me." In a positive response, the disciples "desired to receive him into the boat" (6:21). Whereas the crowd has no idea how Jesus got to the other side of the lake, his disciples do know. Whereas the disciples were in the boat with Jesus and experienced a near theophany, the crowds upon finding Jesus ask simply, "Rabbi, how did you get here?" Thus we have motifs of the Identity and Believing themes in this story. The disciples are the ones who are ready to hear and understand the deeper meaning of the feeding sign. At the end of John 6, it is these disciples who are alone left as Jesus' followers. They are the ones who have recognized Jesus' glory in the previous signs. They are the ones who have believed him and followed him.

The ensuing dialog between Jesus and the crowd is essentially confrontational. The crowd wants more of the same from Jesus (i.e. food) but Jesus desires that they understand the spiritual intent of his sign. As the dialog unfolds we see a complex interaction of all seven themes. Jesus reveals who he is as God, as Savior, as Messiah and as Witness who calls on his listeners to respond in faith and thus secure a future of eternal life rather than judgment.

The dialog of John 6:26–58 consists of three main sections. The first section from 6:28–40 is a sharp back and forth conversation between Jesus and the crowd that concludes with a long response by Jesus. The second section from 6:41–51 begins with reference to the Jews grumbling about the claims of Jesus and proceeds with a second response from Jesus. The third section, 6:52–58, is similar in that it begins by referring to the Jews, this time as fighting among themselves about what Jesus means. Jesus then responds with a third monologue.

WORK FOR THE BREAD THAT REMAINS FOREVER

In response to the question of the crowd, "Rabbi, how did you get here?" (6:25), Jesus totally ignores the question itself and instead upbraids them for their intentions. "You are looking for me not because you saw a sign, but because you ate from the bread and were filled" (6:26). The Believing and Signs themes are on display here. The crowd should be seeking Jesus because they perceived the identity of the one doing the sign. Instead, they were seeking after the benefits of the sign—food. As with the Jewish leaders in chapter 5, here is a second time where a sign does not lead to believing.

Jesus goes on to provoke the crowd with a statement from the Life and Identity themes that does get to the intention of the sign: "Do not work for perishable food, but for food that remains for eternal life, which the Son of Man will give to you" (6:27). "Food" (Gk. *brōsis*) is a little used image that forms part of the Life theme along with water and bread motifs. In John 4:32, Jesus tells the disciples, "I have food to eat that you do not know about." Already, the reader is clued to the symbolic nature of food. Now in 6:27, Jesus places the physical and symbolic in dualistic opposition; he presents a riddle for the crowd to figure out. The source of the food is "the Son of Man." Jesus uses the self-referential phrase common in the Synoptic Gospels. In John, however, the "Son of Man" is a highly theological Identity title conveying Jesus' origin from heaven. Jesus alludes to this meaning by saying, "For God the Father has sealed this one."

The crowd responds with what seems to be a genuine question, "what should we do to work the works of God?" (6:28). They take Jesus' admonition as some type of effort needed to merit the eternal food. And as it stands the statement of Jesus was open to that interpretation. Jesus however explains that the "work" is "to believe in the one whom [God] sent." Jesus invokes the key term for the Believing theme. The "work" is simply to believe in the Son of Man.

The crowd knows that Jesus is speaking about himself: "What sign will you do so we might see and believe you? What work?" (6:30). The crowd's response is not one of believing, but of questioning. As noted in the chapter on the Signs theme, "sign" and "work" are practically synonymous terms in John. Their question exposes a great irony. The previous day the crowd witnessed an unimaginably miraculous event, but either did not perceive or refused to perceive the identity of the one performing the sign. Now they act as if that event meant nothing. From John's theological perspective, we definitely see here that there is no automatic connection between Jesus' performance of a sign and a positive response of believing.

To push their request, the crowd blithely compares this miracle to the giving of manna in the Old Testament. The mention of manna and the timing of the feeding miracle and this conversation as "near the Passover feast" (6:4), clues the reader that the Festival theme is part of the conversation going forward. Jesus' rejoinder makes this clear. In response to the scripture quotation: "he gave them bread to eat from heaven" (6:31, cf. Ps 78:24; Exod 16:4), Jesus corrects their perception with a solemn Witness declaration: "Truly, truly I say to you, Moses did not give you the bread from heaven, but my Father gives you the true bread from heaven" (6:32). In one statement, Jesus sets up a contrast that is typical of the Festival theme. The "true" bread from heaven that "my Father gives" is qualitatively different from the physical bread in the Exodus, notwithstanding its source in God, not Moses. Jesus is speaking of a different bread, the "true" bread, just as he was speaking of a different water to the Samaritan woman.

Jesus continues this thought by speaking about the bread of God with concepts from the Identity and Life themes. First, he states that, "The bread of God is the one who comes down from heaven" (6:33a). "Comes down" (Gk. *katabainō*) is part is the "Descent/Ascent of the Son of Man" motif. The phrase Son of Man appears three times in the context (6:27, 53, 62), a title that Jesus interchanges with "I" throughout. Furthermore, this heavenly bread is the one who gives life to the world (6:33b). Jesus implies that his origin is from the Father and that he brings salvation to the world. The manna of the Israelites has been replaced with the heavenly bread for the world.

Then, in response to another misunderstanding of the crowd ("always give us this bread"), Jesus makes the first of the "I am" with predicate statements in the gospel. Jesus directly equates himself with this bread: "I am the Bread of Life; the one who comes to me will never hunger and the one who believes in me will never thirst" (6:35). This statement is another of the "gospel summaries" akin to 3:16 where John includes at least elements of the Identity, Believing and Destiny themes (see Appendix: The Gospel Summaries in John). In this case, the Life and Festival themes are also present. "I am" corresponds to Identity, "the Bread of Life" to Life (and Festival as counterpart to manna), "come" is the response of the Believing theme, and the positive outcome of the Destiny theme is to never hunger or thirst. John 6 in particular is full of similar statements with varying nuances (see 6:40, 47–48, 51, 53).

The final segment of this section concerns Jesus' response to the unbelieving attitude of the crowd by delving into the Destiny theme. First, Jesus makes a clear assessment of their negative response in 6:36 using Believing language, "But I say to you that you have neither seen me nor believed me." Then Jesus gives a seeming reason for their lack of response, "everyone the Father gives to me comes to me." Further, those who do come can be assured that Jesus will keep them (6:37b) because it is in the Father's will and power to do so in the one he has sent (6:38). We see an element of determinism here as part of the Destiny theme.

Before moving on, I want observe that there is no double-predestination here. Jesus speaks of those who do believe and states the positive proposition that the Father has given those to Jesus and those have indeed come. The converse is never stated that God does not give others into Jesus' hand. There is simply no comment made as to their immediate future. In making this statement, the invitation to believe is always present and incumbent on those present to respond and thus become one of the "all."

The deterministic language of 6:37 continues in 6:39: "This is the will of the one who sent me, that every person he has give me I will not let go from him but will raise him at the last day." Here the Destiny language includes an outcome of eternal life, namely "resurrection." The openness of the invitation to anyone though is evident in 6:40, another "gospel summary" which includes the key themes of Identity, Believing, and Destiny.

"ISN'T THIS JOSEPH'S SON?"

The Jewish crowd listening to Jesus would not accept nor attempt to understand what Jesus said. Instead they "grumbled" at his words. The verb "grumble" (Gk. *goggizō*) recalls the "grumbling" of the Israelites in the wilderness (consistent with the Festival theme manna motif) and is a negative image of the Believing theme. Instead of exploring what Jesus means by his pronouncement, they complain about it and ask an Identity theme question, "Is this not Joseph's son, of whom we know his father and mother? How does he now say 'I have come down from heaven'?" (6:42). John displays irony here, because the reader knows from the Prologue that Jesus' origin is "In the beginning" and that his earthly parentage is of no account. We have another instance of misunderstanding in John.

Jesus implores them not to complain (6:43) and makes another theme-laced observation in 6:44, "no one can come to me (Believing) except the Father who sent me (Witness) draws him (Destiny) and I will raise him (Life) at the last day (Destiny)." Jesus essentially summarizes 6:36–40 here.

Though a deterministic bent appears to drive the statement in 6:44, Jesus continues over the next six verses with a constant invitation to learn and accept his message. In one of the few times in John where the OT is quoted, Jesus tells the crowd, "It is written in the prophets, 'Everyone will be taught by God'" (6:45). The scope of this quotation is universal, not limited. Jesus is telling the crowd that if they would only listen, that they would learn, instead of questioning his every word with a closed mind. If they indeed listen and learn, they will come to Jesus

(6:45). Jesus then makes a series of statements that are thematically rich and repetitive, with instances of the Identity, Life, Festival, Believing and Destiny themes, not to mention that the images of bread and eating hark back to the sign at the start of John 6. With regard to Identity, Jesus tells them in 6:46, "Not that anyone has seen the Father except the one who is from God; he has seen the Father." There is an allusion to 1:18 here. Jesus also speaks again of his descent from heaven (6:50, 51) and thus his origin.

Life is the dominant theme in this passage revolving around the image of bread and the divine action of giving life. In fact, in 6:48, Jesus repeats 6:35, "I am the Bread of Life" and then modifies the phrase in 6:51 with "I am the living Bread." In himself, Jesus has life (cf. 1:4) and offers that life to those who will partake of it. What is more, however, Jesus makes the identification of the Bread of Life extremely vivid and specific when he makes the astounding statement in 6:51 that "the bread which I will give is my flesh for the life of the world." Jesus "gives" the bread, just as God has "given" his Son (3:16), and Jesus "gives" living water (4:10, 14) and "eternal life" (6:27). What Jesus gives here is "my flesh." The *Logos* become flesh now says he will give that very flesh for the life of the world. The image is not yet defined, though John has referred to the destruction of the "temple of his body" in 2:21. Ultimately we know that giving his "flesh" refers the cross where Jesus "lays down his life" (10:11). Furthermore, this gift of his flesh is for the life of the "world" which stands arrayed against him. The absolute love of God is in evidence here. The "flesh" image introduced here becomes part of the image pair of "flesh" and "blood" in 6:52–59.

Jesus proclamation, "I am the Bread of Life" in 6:48 takes on a Festival theme layer when followed by the contrasting statements of 6:49–50: "your fathers ate manna in the wilderness and died; this is the bread coming down from heaven, so that whoever eats from it also will never die." Manna is only an imperfect physical food that is now replaced with the eternal food of the Bread of Life.

Throughout this section verbs from the Believing theme occur multiple times including hear, learn, come, see, believe, and eat. The invitation to act comes in varied images that ultimately mean one thing: believe in Jesus. The most vivid and provocative of these is the verb "eat." The hearers are invited to eat the bread—but the bread is Jesus' flesh. This connection becomes the basis for the argument in the final section.

Wedded to several of these verbs are positive Destiny images including "eternal life" with believe (6:47), "will never die" with eat (6:50), and "will live forever" with eat (6:51). The final Destiny image is perhaps the most profound one; Jesus gives his flesh for "the life of the world." This "life" is the outcome of eternal life that is based in the life-giving action of Jesus. The outcome is only a potential one, however, because "the world" must respond with belief.

"UNLESS YOU EAT MY FLESH . . ."

The third and final section of the "Bread of Life" discourse begins with another notice of discontent. This time the Jews "argued with one another" about how Jesus could "give us his flesh to eat?" (6:52). Here is another instance of misunderstanding that sets the stage for Jesus' symbolic treatment of "eating flesh" and "drinking blood." The ensuing words from Jesus may be the most difficult in the gospel to apprehend, particularly for the listeners in the story.

Jesus takes the question from the Jews and pushes their understanding to its limits and beyond. He begins in 6:53 with a Witness statement that is the gospel message in negative form: "Truly, truly I say to you, unless you eat the flesh of the Son of Man and drink his blood you have no life in yourselves." The structure is akin to Jesus' statement to Nicodemus, "Unless a person is born from above, he cannot see the kingdom of God." Here, however, the action is expected from the hearers; they must "eat the flesh" and "drink the blood" of the Son of Man. We as readers can immediately detect the symbolic nature of eating and drinking because they are Believing theme verbs whose objects are the Life images (flesh and blood) of the "Son of Man" (Identity) and whose outcome is the Destiny phrase of "life in yourselves" (i.e. eternal life). "Eating his flesh" and "drinking his blood" are metaphors for believing in the salvific effects of Christ's death on the cross (cf. 19:34–35). John's first readers almost certainly saw a direct reference to the Christian Eucharist or Lord's Supper. Interestingly, John does not include the eating of the bread and wine in his telling of the Last Supper, but instead includes the washing of the disciples' feet. John may well have seen Jesus' words here in John 6 as the only ones necessary for his reader's to connect to the meaning of their communion practice. For the audience in the story, however, the graphic images Jesus presented were almost too much to bear or understand from their concrete perspective and perception.

The "unless . . . not" statement of 6:53 is followed immediately with a straightforward restatement in 6:54, "the one who eats my flesh and drinks my blood has eternal life" but with the additional Destiny statement, "and I will raise him at the last day." The connection between the present outcome of "has eternal life" and the future outcome of "I will raise him at the last day" is an example of John's "continuous eschatology."

In what is another Festival theme contrast using Witness language, Jesus goes on to develop the symbolism: "for my flesh is true food and my blood is true drink." Physical food and drink, even manna or water from the rock, meet only physical life needs. Jesus' flesh and blood is authentic ("true") spiritual food.

The final three verses bring the entirety of the discourse to a thematic summation that repeats previous material but in slightly new formulations. In a look forward to the Believing theme language of the farewell speeches in 13–16, Jesus tells the listeners that, "the one who eats my flesh and drinks my blood *remains* in me and I in him" (6:56). There is a unity between the believer and Jesus when the believer partakes. There is a further connection with the Father, because it is "the living Father who sent me" (6:57; Witness theme); as a result "the one eating me will also live through me." There is a Life connection between the Father, the Son and the one who believes (partakes of) the Son, resulting in life (Destiny).

The last verse packs together the Identity, Life, Festival, Believing and Destiny themes in one final way: "this is the Bread that comes down from heaven, not as the fathers ate and died; the one eating this Bread will live forever" (6:58). I trust that you now can easily see each theme in this statement!

CONCLUSION

In many and varied ways, John 6:26–58 has presented and woven together all the themes in the gospel. The theme seemingly least represented, the Signs theme, may in fact be the ultimately dominating one. In 6:30, the crowd asked, "What sign are you doing, that we should see and believe you." Throughout the rest of the passage Jesus presents himself as *the* sign, as the true bread pointed to by the bread of the initial miracle. In keeping with the main focus of the Signs theme, John explores whether the audience in the story will recognize the sign and move to belief.

In this instance, the answer is largely negative. Not only do we see the crowd grumbling and arguing over what Jesus says about himself, but in the aftermath, even many of Jesus' disciples found what he said difficult (6:60). Jesus goes on to explain "It is the Spirit that gives life; the flesh is of no benefit. The words which I have spoken are spirit and are life" (6:63). He says outright that they need to take what he has said symbolically not literally. Despite Jesus' remark, he himself recognized those who would not believe (6:64) and explains this situation with another deterministic statement (6:65). And indeed, many then left him (6:66). The sign and Jesus' interpretation of the sign proved to be lost on the many in the crowd and even his disciples. Only a few remained who truly believed. Peter represents their positive and on-going response with his confession, "Lord, to whom shall we go, you have the words of eternal life, and we have believed and we know that you are the Holy One of God" (6:68–69). Peter has moved beyond "signs faith" to a deeply authentic faith in Jesus that proves to endure despite his later denials in the passion.

10

A Thematic Analysis of John 17

THE LORD'S PRAYER MAY be the most well known prayer of Jesus, but the prayer of Jesus in John 17 arguably surpasses the Lord's Prayer in its theological depth. In its chronological place, John 17 occurs at roughly the same time as the prayer in Gethsemane of the Synoptic gospels, but very different in content except for the deep desire to carry out the desires of the Father. Jesus' prayer in John 17 is the conclusion to the major section of John that runs from chapters 13 to 17. In John 2–12, Jesus carried out a public ministry, but from 13–17 Jesus exclusively speaks to his disciples. In John 13–16 Jesus prepares the disciples for the future by giving them an example of service, by predicting the soon to be carried out events surrounding the passion, by discussing the necessity of his departure, by telling them of the gift of the Holy Spirit-Paraclete, and by bluntly stating the persecution to come and the power they possessed to overcome the persecution. He calls on his disciples to love one another and to stay intimately connected to himself, "the Vine." The themes of Identity, Life, Witness, Believing, and Destiny are all prominent in these chapters. The implementation of the themes is slightly different from the first half of John, however, for Jesus is not trying to convince people to believe, but now he is preparing those who have believed for the future.

In John 17, Jesus turns attention from the disciples to God. There is no indication that the disciples are not present; to the contrary, the prayer is to God on their behalf in their presence. Jesus' prayer is above all a prayer focused on unity between the Father, the Son, and those who believe in the Son for the ultimate purpose of a witness to the world. The prayer divides roughly into three sections. The first focuses on the relation of the Son to the Father and the completion of the Son's mission (17:1–8); the second is Jesus prayer for the disciples proper (17:9–18);

133

the third is a prayer for future disciples and for the world (17:20–26). The style of Jesus words is very consistent with the preceding discourses in John. As such thematic analysis works well; the whole is tightly woven with threads from the various themes in the Gospel, including Identity, Life, Witness, Believing, Signs, and Destiny. The Festival theme is faintly evident.

"THE HOUR HAS COME"

Jesus begins the prayer with an intense understanding of his own Destiny, wedded to the Identity and Life themes. He addresses God as "Father" (Gk. *pater*) throughout (17:1, 5, 11, 21, 24, 25); by doing so Jesus claims a familial identification with God. He prays, "Father, the hour has come, glorify your son, so that the Son may glorify you." John 17 is the culmination of the "hour" motif that began in chapter two and periodically appears at various places in the first twelve chapters as not yet come (2:4; 7:30; 8:20). In 12:23, Jesus says in similar language: "The hour has come for the Son of Man to be glorified." He follows on that statement in 12:27–29 with "Now my soul is troubled, and what should I say; Father, save me from this hour? But I came for this. Father, glorify your name." In a voice from heaven, the Father then affirms in 12:28 "I have glorified and I will glorify." Chapter 13 begins with a similar understanding of the impending hour of destiny: "Jesus, knowing that his hour had come to pass from this world to the Father . . ." Now, at the moment of the passion, which John styles as Jesus' "lifting up" or "glorification," Jesus places this destined moment fully within the bounds of his relationship with the Father in 17:1. God glorifies Jesus in their mutual consent that the cross is the place where Jesus will bring maximum glory to the Father.

The continuation in 17:2 has slightly deterministic language: "just as you have given him authority over all flesh, so that all you have given him, he might give to them eternal life." The Father-Son relationship is deeply maintained in that the Father gives to the Son the prerogatives of life and judgment (John 5), and more specifically that the Father grants those to whom Jesus gives eternal life. Jesus as Life is the one who actually gives life. The cross (the focal point of Jesus' "hour") is the point whereby Jesus' authority over all flesh is realized. There, at the lifting up of the Son of Man, Jesus draws all people to himself "so that all who believe might have eternal life" (3:14–15; 12:32).

Lest an absolute determinism take over the thought here, Jesus defines eternal life in 17:3: "that they know you the only true God and the one you sent, Jesus Christ." The response of people in acknowledging God and Christ together is essential to this gift of eternal life (Believing theme). While the language here tends toward the role of God in the process, John always reminds the reader that our response is involved.

The object of "know" is set out with a combination of Identity and Witness language. Though implied throughout, the designation "only God" is found only here in 17:3 and 5:44, and only here with "true." Jewish monotheism shines through here but in combination with the confession of Jesus Christ as fully part of who God is. The descriptor "and whom you sent, Jesus Christ" expresses Identity, Witness and even the Festival themes in that Jesus Christ is set in combination with God (Identity), is sent from God (Witness) and is rendered as "Christ," the Jewish Messiah (Festival).

In 17:4 and 5, Jesus proclaims a statement of obedience to the mission of God and presents a petition. Jesus states that, "I have glorified you on the earth by completing the work that you gave me to do." On the eve of the cross, Jesus looks back on what he has already accomplished using a combination of Witness language—"I have glorified you on the earth"—and the Signs theme with reference to Jesus' "work." This statement of obedience is the basis for the Identity language of Jesus' request, "now glorify me, Father, with the glory from yourself which I had from you before the world existed" (17:5).

The most repeated word in this first section is "glorify" (Gk. *doxazō*), where it occurs 5 times of the 22 total in John. John uses "glorify" in a variety of contexts and more interestingly connects the term to a number of themes. The basic idea of "glorify" is to render high reputation or honor to someone (cf. 8:54). The Father primarily "glorifies" Jesus in the cross and resurrection (Destiny; cf. 7:39, 12:16; 13:31–32; 17:1a); Jesus glorifies the Father by completing his work which would include his "signs" and his impending death (so Witness+Signs+Destiny; cf. 11:4; 17:1b, 4; also "glory" in 2:11); Jesus prays for God to glorify him with the glory he had before the world existed (Identity, cf. 1:14 "glory as of the only-begotten of the Father"). This multi-themed word reminds us that context is all-important in assessing an image or term. John is subtle and complex in this regard.

Since Jesus refers to his followers, some see 17:6–8 as the beginning of the next section. But the tone of the verses continues the claims of Jesus with regard to completing the work of the Father, using the language of Witness, Believing, Identity, and Destiny. Jesus clearly states his witness in 17:6: "I have revealed your name to the people whom you gave me from the world." What Jesus reveals is the name of God. This "name" may refer to the "I am" Jesus uses throughout the gospel, but in a broader sense, Jesus "has made [the Father] known" (1:18) in all of his words and actions. Once again there is a predestinarian cast to "the people whom you gave me." The next phrase only adds to this connotation, "They were yours and you gave them to me." Nonetheless the basis for the statement is that "they have kept your word." The response of "keeping" is the indicator of their identity in God. Jesus affirms their "knowing" based on his witness: "now they know that everything you have given to me is from you because I have given to them the words you gave to me" (17:7–8a). Along with "keep" and "know," John strings together a series of Believing terms in the final phases, "and they *received* . . . and they *knew* truly . . . and they *believed* . . . " (17:8). What they know is Jesus' identity ("I have come from you"); what they believe is that "you sent me."

"HOLY FATHER, KEEP THEM"

In the last two thirds of the chapter, Jesus moves from a focus on his accomplishment of the Father's work to prayers for the disciples (17:9–19) and others (17:20–26). He begins the first part with a series of petitions for his own followers in light of his impending departure (17:11, 13, "I am coming to you"). The entire section is an amalgam of thematic elements intended to highlight a request for unity between the Father, the Son and the disciples, despite the disciples continued presence in the world. This unity is intended as preparation for their mission in the world.

The initiation of the request section highlights the distinct destinies of the disciples and the world, respectively: "I am asking concerning them; I am not asking concerning the world." From John 13 onwards, the term "world" (Gk. *kosmos*) usually represents collectively those who have rejected Jesus. This stance of the world is certainly the case in John 17, except for general references to creation in 17:5, 24. The difference in destinies is reinforced throughout the section. Jesus refers to the disciples as "those you have given me, because they are yours" (17:9, also vv. 11, 12, 24). The world, however, "hated them" (17:14). The contrast is evident in 17:14 and 16: "[the disciples] are not from the world, just as I am not from the world." But one cannot say that the destiny of every individual in the world is yet determined. Indeed, part of the mission of the disciples is "so that the world might know that you sent them and that you loved them just as you loved me (17:23)." The world in general terms, however, stands against God's own and thus lies in judgment.

For the disciples, they now have a new identity; they are now from the same place Jesus is. They now belong to God. Jesus' petition for unity is based in the unity of the Father and Son and their mutual possession of the disciples (17:10, "what is mine is yours and what is yours is mine, and I have been glorified in them"). Thus Jesus prays in 17:11, "keep them in your name, whom you gave to me, so they might be one just as we are." Their new identity is to result in unity. Thus far Jesus has accomplished this task of unity with his presence, except for Judas (v. 12). Now that Jesus returns to the Father, Jesus prays that the Father would accomplish the task.

As elements of this unity Jesus asks that God "would keep them from the evil one" (17:5) and "sanctify them in the truth" (17:17). These requests for unity, keeping from evil, and consecration are all related to the mission of the disciples (Witness theme).[1] When Jesus leaves, the disciples are still "in the world" (17:11). The verb "consecrate" or "sanctify" (Gk. *agiazō*) is rare in John (only 10:36; 17:17, 19). The idea of the term is "to set apart" for a task. In 10:36, Jesus is "the one the Father has sanctified and sent into the world." The thought here is the same. Jesus prays for his disciples to be sanctified in the truth for mission to the world as 17:18 clearly sets out: "Just as you sent me into the world, I also have sent them into the world." After the resurrection, Jesus actually commissions the disciples with similar words, "As the Father has sent me, I also am sending you" (20:21). But Jesus does not just leave the task of consecration to the Father, but he too participates: "On their behalf, I am sanctifying myself, so that they might also be sanctified in the truth." Jesus refers here to his impending death, resurrection and return to God as the means for empowering the disciples for their task.

There is one clear instance of the Festival theme in this section; in this case it does not have to do with Jesus but with Judas, the betrayer of Jesus. After Jesus' claims that he has kept, guarded and not lost any that the Father has given him in 17:12, he adds "except the son of

---

1. Cf. Barrett, *St. John*, 510–11.

destruction so that scripture might be fulfilled." The specific scripture referred to is probably the one from Ps. 41:10 that Jesus quotes in 13:18. The NRSV renders "son of destruction" as "the one destined to be lost," which is perhaps too specific. Notably, Judas is not named, but referred to in theological terms. While Judas was the actual fulfillment, it is at least debatable that he only and not another must have been the "son of destruction." Judas chose to betray Jesus.

"ALSO FOR THOSE BELIEVING THROUGH THEIR WORD"

The final section continues Jesus' intercessory prayer. The thematic material is largely the same using motifs repeated earlier in the prayer. Up until this point in the gospel, those believing in Jesus have largely done so because of Jesus' words and actions. In this section it is "their word," that is the witness of the disciples, that will lead to a believing response in Jesus. So Jesus now turns his petitions from his disciples to those who will believe in the future, "for those who believe in me through their word" (17:20). Implicit in Jesus' request is the assumption that the witness of the disciples will result in a successful mission.

The first petition is a second and expanded prayer for unity (Identity): "I ask . . . that all might be one, just as you Father are in me and I in you so that they might be in us" (17:21). In previous sections of the gospel, Jesus has spoken of his identification with the Father in similar terms, for example, "believe my works, so you might know and keep knowing that I am in the Father and the Father is in me" (10:38; cf. 14:10–11). In 14:20, Jesus even includes his disciples in these words of mutual dwelling. Now, he includes all future followers in the triadic circle of indwelling.

As in the previous section, the new identity is the basis for a successful mission to the world, "so that the world might believe that you sent me." Here is where the prayer comes closest to John 3:16. God gave his Son so that all might believe. Now it is the unified followers of Jesus who witness to that message in the world. Though the world as a whole rejects the message, Jesus' followers still proclaim the message with the hope that some from that world will respond in belief. Those who have believed now become agents of revelation to the world.

Jesus not only prays that the Father will bring unity but says that he himself will participate in bringing unity also. Jesus "has given them the glory which you gave me, so they might be one as we are one" (17:22).

The purpose is the same but expanded, "so the world might know that you sent me and you loved them [i.e. the disciples] just as you loved me" (17:23). The Believing theme is reiterated with a change to the verb "know." For John believing and knowing are essentially synonymous. The implication here is that when believers are unified with the character and purposes of God, the world recognizes something amazing, that God loves those who are following Jesus in the same way he loves Jesus. The Destiny theme appears here; those whose destiny is eternal life becomes evident to those whose destiny is not, so that by God's grace their destiny will change to eternal life. In so doing they too will experience God's love as love and not judgment.

The last verses of the prayer include the verb "love" (Gk. *agapaō*) four times (as well as the noun *agapē*). These uses are part of a motif that begins in John 3:16 and is concentrates in John 13–16. Like the Spirit motif and several others, "love" crosses several themes. Where "the Father loves the Son" we see the Identity theme (3:35; 5:20—using Gk. *phileō*; 10:17; 15:9; 17:23, 24, 26). These uses indicate the deep, unbreakable familial bond between the Father and Son. Jesus extends this love to his disciples, whom he now calls "friends" (15:13). Love for his friends means laying his life for them. This "love" is connected to the Life theme, the same love we find in John 3:16. In 17:23, Father-Son love and the love for the disciples are set together: "So the world might know that you . . . loved them just as you loved me." The Father loves those belonging to the Son in the same way he loves the Son.

In the final three verses, Jesus' prayer looks to the future. Despite similar language to the rest of the prayer, the scope has changed. When Jesus prays in 17:24, "Father, my desire for those you have given me is that where I am going, they might be with me," he is now speaking not only of the current disciples, but the future ones who will come from the world. Jesus' desire is that their destiny will be with him. His reason for desiring their presence is so that they can see (or behold, Gk. *theoreō*) the entirety of Jesus' glory; not just the time-space evidence of that glory in the signs and in the passion-resurrection to come, but the "glory that you gave to me because you loved me before the foundation of the world" (17:24). The experience of this glory is yet to come for those who believe. Jesus acknowledges in 17:25 that these believers now know that the Father sent Jesus, in distinction to the world, which does not. Finally,

Jesus professes that he has made God's name known (Witness) so that God's love might be in them.

With the inclusion of Jesus' prayer in John 17, John has brought together all the key themes of the gospel in a way that provides a bridge from the present completion of his ministry through the passion and to the future. Jesus as "the only-begotten God who is in the bosom of the Father" has indeed made God known and now passes that task on to those who believe in him.

Epilogue

Beyond the Themes

T*HE GOSPEL OF JOHN: A Thematic Approach* has been all about help-
ing you, the reader, see what John is doing in his gospel. With the
tools of the thematic approach, you should now be able to read John
with new eyes. How does every story in John tell the theological story
of Jesus? You should now be able to see how the themes interact with
one another to build John's theology of how God revealed himself in the
Logos, Jesus Christ, and how John calls on people to respond.

But the identification of the themes and their interactions are only
the beginning steps for delving into the theology of John. At points in
this book, I have tried to contribute to aspects of John's theology, especially in the Destiny theme, but in every case my comments are only
a starting point. I see this book as a companion to commentaries and
other studies and not as a substitute. The commentaries listed in the
bibliography will take the one who studies them deeper into individual
sections of the gospel with more extended analyses of the language and
context of those passages. Some commentaries almost require some
knowledge of Greek, such as those by Barrett and Beasley-Murray, but
most are accessible with only knowledge of English. Different commentaries focus on different aspects of John from a highly detailed emphasis
on history and background (such as Brown and Keener) to others that
are more focused on the literary plan of John and his theology (such as
Carson, Morris and Ridderbos). A few give a nice balance between the
two (Barrett and Borchert are examples). In addition to commentaries,
there are some very good treatments of John's symbolism and theology,
notably the works by Koester, D. M. Smith, and Köstenberger. I have
already mentioned the exemplary work of Kysar in the Introduction.
Each of non-commentary studies in the bibliography makes a distinct
contribution to an understanding of John's theology.

Beyond additional study, however, my hope is that your understanding of the themes in John will lead you to consider in a deeper way the claims of John and how they make a claim on your life and the lives of others. My greatest desire is that you will be a participant in the purpose of John to experience the love of God and to speak the love of God to the world.

Appendix

The Gospel Summaries in John

R EADERS OF JOHN HAVE long noted that their are two distinct summaries of the Gospel message in the gospel, John 3:16 and John
20:30–31. In fact, there are quite a few more. In keeping with John's
strategy to present the whole of the gospel message at numerous points
in the gospel, close observation shows that there are at least thirteen of
these summaries in the gospel (one could argue for others). Each gospel summary contains at a minimum the themes of Identity, Believing,
and Destiny. Each summary usually begins with themes of Revelation
(Identity/Life/Festival/Witness), has some sort of conditional statement
involving the Believing theme, and concludes with outcomes of the
Destiny theme.

John 3:16 Identity, Life, Believing, Destiny

John 3:36 Identity, Believing, Destiny

John 4:14 Identity, Life, Believing, Destiny

John 5:24 Identity, Witness, Believing, Destiny

John 6:35 (51, 53–54, 58) Identity, Life (and Festival), Believing,
Destiny

John 8:12 Identity, Life (and Festival), Believing, Destiny

John 10:9 Identity, Life, Believing, Destiny

John 11:25–26 Identity, Life, Believing, Destiny

John 12:46–48 Identity, Life, Believing, Destiny

John 20:30–31 Identity, Festival, Believing, Signs, Destiny

Bibliography

Ashton, John. "The Transformation of Wisdom." In *Studying John: Approaches to the Fourth Gospel*, 5–35. New York: Oxford University Press, 1998.

Barrett, C. K. *The Gospel According to St. John*. 2nd ed. Philadelphia: Westminster, 1978.

———. *Essays on John*. Philadelphia: Westminster, 1982.

Bauckham, Richard, and Carl Mosser. *The Gospel of John and Christian Theology*. Grand Rapids: Eerdmans, 2008.

Beasley-Murray, George R. *John*. Word Biblical Commentary, 36. Waco, TX: Word, 1987.

———. *Word Biblical Themes: John*. Waco, TX: Word, 1989.

———. *Gospel of Life: Theology in the Fourth Gospel*. Peabody, MA: Hendrickson, 1991.

Borchert, Gerald L. *John 1–11*. Nashville: Broadman & Holman, 1996.

———. *John 12–21*. Nashville: Broadman & Holman, 2002.

Brown, Raymond. *The Gospel According to John*. The Anchor Bible Commentary. Vols. 29 and 29a. New Haven, CT: Yale University Press, 1966–1970.

Bultmann, Rudolf. *Theology of the New Testament*. Waco, TX: Baylor University Press, 2007.

Burge, Gary M. *John*. NIV Application Commentary. Grand Rapids: Zondervan, 2000.

Carson, D. A. *The Gospel According to John*. Grand Rapids: Eerdmans, 1991.

Culpepper, R. Alan. *Anatomy of the Fourth Gospel*. Philadelphia: Fortress, 1983.

Dodd, C. H. *The Interpretation of the Fourth Gospel*. Cambridge: Cambridge University Press, 1968.

Frey, Jorg, Jan G. Van Der Watt, Ruben Zimmermann, and Gabi Kern. *Imagery in the Gospel of John: Terms, Forms, Themes and Theology of Johannine Figurative Language*. Untersuchungen Zum Neuen Testament. Tübingen: Mohr Siebeck, 2006.

Hoskyns, Edwyn, and Noel Davies. *The Fourth Gospel*. London: Faber and Faber, 1947.

Keener, Craig S. *The Gospel of John: A Commentary*. 2 vols. Peabody, MS: Hendrickson, 2004.

Koester, Craig R. *Symbolism in the Fourth Gospel: Meaning, Mystery, Community*. 2nd ed. Minneapolis: Fortress, 2003.

———. *The Word of Life: A Theology of John's Gospel*. Grand Rapids: Eerdmans, 2008.

Köstenberger, Andreas. *Encountering John: The Gospel in Historical, Literary, and Theological Perspective*. Grand Rapids: Baker, 2002.

———. *A Theology of John's Gospel and Letters: The Word, the Christ, the Son of God*. Grand Rapids: Zondervan, 2009.

Kysar, Robert. *John, the Maverick Gospel*. 3rd ed. Louisville, KY: Westminster/John Knox, 2007.

Lindars, Barnabus. *The Gospel of John*. Atlanta: John Knox, 1972.

———. *John*. Sheffield: Sheffield Academic Press, 1990.

Morris, Leon. *The Gospel According to John*. Grand Rapids: Eerdmans, 1971.

Neyrey, Jerome. *The Gospel of John*. New Cambridge Bible Commentary. New York: Cambridge University Press, 2007.

Ridderbos, Herman. *The Gospel of John: A Theological Commentary*. Grand Rapids: Eerdmans, 1997.

Rowland, Christopher. "The Mystical Element in the Gospels and Acts." In Christopher Rowland and Christopher R. A. Murray-Jones, *The Mystery of God*, 123–131. Leiden: Brill, 2009.

Smith, Dwight Moody. *The Theology of the Gospel of John*. Cambridge: Cambridge University Press, 1995.

Scripture Index